J.P. Morris

A Glossary of the Words and Phrases of Furness

Salzwasser

J.P. Morris

A Glossary of the Words and Phrases of Furness

1. Auflage | ISBN: 978-3-84605-280-8

Erscheinungsort: Frankfurt, Deutschland

Erscheinungsjahr: 2020

Salzwasser Verlag GmbH

Reprint of the original, first published in 1869.

A GLOSSARY

OF THE

WORDS AND PHRASES OF FURNESS.

A GLOSSARY

OF THE

Words and Phrases of Furness

(NORTH LANCASHIRE,)

*With Illustrative Quotations, principally
from the Old Northern Writers.*

BY

J. P. MORRIS, F. A. S. L.

CORR. MEM. ANTH. SOC. OF PARIS.

"Hyt semeth a gret wondur hough Englysch that
ys the burth-tonge of Englyschemen and here oune
longage and tonge ys so dyvers of soun in this ylond."
—*Higden's Polychronicon*, trans. by JOHN DE TREVISA,
A.D. 1387.

LONDON: J. RUSSELL SMITH.
CARLISLE: GEO. COWARD.
MDCCCLXIX.

TO

HIS GRACE THE DUKE OF DEVONSHIRE,

K.G., &c., &c.,

THESE PAGES ARE (BY PERMISSION)

RESPECTFULLY DEDICATED,

BY HIS

OBLIGED AND HUMBLE SERVANT,

THE AUTHOR.

PREFACE.

In presenting the following pages as a humble contribution to the literature of Lancashire, it is far from the Author's intention to assume to himself the mantle of the philologist. The work, begun as an amusement, has been carried on to its conclusion mainly for the purpose of rescuing from oblivion a few of the good old forms of speech which are now fast becoming obsolete; and also as a means whereby some of the obscure phrases of our early English writers may possibly be elucidated. Take for instance the following :—

"In heuene cometh no foolis *to yeere.*"

.   .   .   .

"Wenest thou with thin hond heuene to reche?
Thin arme wole not be so longe *to yeere.*"

Both these passages occur in *Hymns to the Virgin and Christ*, edited by Mr. Furnivall, for the Early English Text Society, and are thus *doubtfully* glossed :—"? A.S. *yeare,* certainly." But, *ta-yeere* is as commonly used in Furness at the present time as it was by the writer of the above lines in A.D. 1430, and by Chaucer in A.D. 1380. Literally its meaning is—*this year;* and the same phrase is also used metaphorically for *a long time,* or *never.*

Although on the title page this work is designated *A Glossary of the Words and Phrases of Furness,* it is by no means intended to imply that many of the words are not in use elsewhere. Most of them, subject to slight orthographical changes, are found in all counties in which the great Northumbrian dialect was once spoken; and others, especially those of Anglo-Saxon origin, are found in widely separated parts of the country.

In prosecuting his studies, and in the preparation of this volume, many and varied were the acts of kindness the Author received at the hands of gentlemen interested in dialectical and early English literature, chief amongst whom he may mention—Edwin Waugh, the "Lancashire Poet;" the late J. Harland; the Rev. Geo. G. Perry, M.A., editor of *Morte Arthure;* Albert Way, Esq., M.A., editor of *Promptorium Parvulorum;* Richard Morris, Esq., the eminent Chaucerian scholar; and the Rev. W. W. Skeat, M.A., editor of *Piers Plowman.*

To the latter two gentlemen more especially are his thanks due for the many valuable suggestions, corrections, and additions made to the work as the sheets passed through the press.

In conclusion, no one can be more conscious of his short-comings than the Author himself; and notwithstanding every care has been taken to exclude errors, many will no doubt have unavoidably crept in; but in the words of Richard Rolle De Hampole he would say :—

> " And if any man that es clerk,
>   Can fynde any errour in this werk,
>   I pray hym he do me that favour,
>   That he wille amende that errour;
>   For if men may here any erroure se,
>   Or if any defaut in this tretice be,
>   I make here a protestacion,
>   That I wil stand til the correccion
>   Of ilka rightwyse lered man,
>   That my defaut here correcte can."

22, SANDSTONE ROAD,
  OLD SWAN, LIVERPOOL.

*List of Abbreviations and Titles of Books
consulted or quoted.*

———

A.S.   Anglo-Saxon.
Celt.   Celtic.
Cf.   *confer*, compare.
Dan.   Danish.
Du.   Dutch.
Fr.   French.
Gael.   Gaelic.
Germ.   German.
Icel.   Icelandic.
Lat.   Latin.
Moes. G.   Moeso-Gothic.
N.   Norse.
O.N.   Old Norse.
O.E.   Old English.
Sc.   Scottish.
Su. G.   Suio-Gothic.
Sw.   Swedish.
W.   Welsh.

Allit. P. "Early English Alliterative Poems in the West Midland Dialect (Lancashire) of the 14th Cent." Edited by Richard Morris, Esq. (Early English Text Society) 1864. This volume contains three poems, which are quoted as A, B, C.

Cant. Tales. The Canterbury Tales of Geoffry Chaucer. Edited by Thos. Wright, Esq., M.A. (No date.) The numbering of the lines correspond with Tyrwhitt's edition.

Hamp. Prose Treats. "English Prose Treatises of Richard Rolle De Hampole (who Died A.D. 1349.)" Edited by the Rev. Geo. G. Perry, M.A. (Early English Text Society, 1866.)

Hymns to Virg. & Christ. "Hymns to the Virgin and Christ, The Parliament of Devils, and other Religious Poems." Edited by F. J. Furnivall, M.A. (Early English Text Society, 1867.)

"Lancelot of the Laik : a Scottish Metrical Romance about 1490—1500 A.D." Edited by the Rev. W. W. Skeat, M.A. (Early English Text Society, 1865.)

Morte Arthure. Edited, from Robert Thornton's M.S., by the Rev. Geo. G. Perry, M.A. (Early English Text Society, 1865.)

Orth. & Con. Brit. Tongue. Of the Orthographie and Congruitie of the Britan Tongue. Edited by H. B. Wheatley. (Early English Text Society, 1865.)

P. of Consc.   The Pricke of Conscience (stimulus conscientiæ) : a Northumbrian Poem by Richard Rolle De Hampole (circa 1345 A.D.).   Edited for the Philological Society by Richard Morris, Esq., 1863.

Piers. Plow.   The Vision of William concerning Piers Plowman, by William Langland.   A.D. 1362.   Edited, from the Vernon M.S., by the Rev. W. W. Skeat, M.A.   (Early English Text Society, 1867.)

Pierce the Ploughman's Crede, (about 1394 A.D.) to which is appended God Spede the Plough, (about 1500 A.D.)   Edited by the Rev. W. W. Skeat, M.A.   (Early English Text Society, 1867.)

Pol. Rel. & Love P.   Political, Religious, & Love Poems.   Edited by F. J. Furnivall, Esq., M.A. (Early English Text Society, 1866.)

Rel. Ant.   Reliquiæ Antiquæ ; Scraps from Ancient Manuscripts, Illustrating chiefly Early English Literature, &c.   Edited by Thos. Wright, Esq., M.A., and Jas. Orchard Halliwell, Esq., F.R.S. 2 vols.   London, 1843.

Relig. Pieces.   Religious Pieces in Prose and Verse. Edited, from Robert Thornton's M.S. (circa 1440), by the Rev. Geo. G. Perry, M.A.

Sp. E. Eng.   Specimens of Early English, selected from the chief English Authors, A.D. 1250— A.D. 1400.   By R. Morris, Esq.   Oxford, 1867.

The Avow. K. Arth.   Three Early English Metrical Romances (about 1300 A.D.), containing "The Anters of Arther at the Tarnewathelan," "Sir Amadace," and "The Avowynge of King Arther, Sir Gawan, Sir Kaye, and Sir Bawdewyn of Bretan." Edited by John Robson, Esq. (Camden Society, 1842.)

The Works of William Shakespeare (Globe edition)

The Lonsdale Magazine.   3 vols.   Kirkby Lonsdale, 1820-2.

The North Lonsdale Magazine.   Ulverstone, 1867.

The Lancashire Dialect, Illustrated in Two Lectures by the Rev. W. Gaskell, M.A.   London, 1854.

Cumb. Ball.   The Songs and Ballads of Cumberland. London, 1866.

Lanc. Ball.   Ballads and Songs of Lancashire, chiefly older than the 19th Cent.   By J. Harland. London, 1865.

Tufts of Heather from the Northern Moors.   By Edwin Waugh.   London (no date).

Sketches of Lancashire Life and Localities.   By Edwin Waugh.   London, 1857.

Lancashire Songs.   By Edwin Waugh.   London, 1866.

Alfred Staunton.   By J. S. Bigg.   London, 1858.

Shifting Scenes, and other Poems.   By J. S. Bigg.
London, 1862.

The Nursery Rhymes of England.   By J. O.
Halliwell.   5th edition.   London (no date).

Percy's Reliques of Ancient English Poetry (Bohn's
edition.)   London, 1845.

Sp. West. Dial.   Specimens of the Westmorland
Dialect.   Kendal, 1868.

Three Furness Dialect Stories :—"Siege o'
Brou'ton," "Lebby Beck Dobby," and "Invasion o' U'ston."   Carlisle, 1868.

A Dictionary of the First or Oldest Words in the
English Language, from A.D. 1250 to 1300.   By
the late Herbert Coleridge.   London, 1863.

A Compendious Anglo-Saxon and English Dictionary.   By the Rev. Joseph Bosworth, D.D.,
&c.   London, 1868.

An Etymological Dictionary of the Scottish Language.   By John Jamieson, D.D.   Edinburgh,
1818.

Dialect of Banffshire, with a Glossary of Words
not in Jamieson's Scottish Dictionary.   By the
Rev. Walter Gregor.   Philological Society, 1866.

Hall.   A Dictionary of Archaic and Provincial Words.
By J. O. Halliwell.   2 vols.   London, 1865.

Chambers's Etymological Dictionary of the English Language. London, 1867.

A Glossary of the Cleveland Dialect. By the Rev. J. C. Atkinson. London, 1868.

A Short Handbook of Comparative Philology. By Hyde Clarke, D.C.L. London, 1859.

Prompt. Parv. Promptorium Parvulorum Sive Clericorum, Dictionarius Anglo-Latinus Princeps. Circa 1440. Edited by Albert Way, Esq., M.A. (Camden Society, 1865.)

Dansk og Engelsk Haand-Lexicon af Christian Friderich Bay. Copenhagen, 1824.

Tauchnitz' Pocket Dictionary of the English and Dutch Languages. Leipsic.

French-English Dictionary. By Alfred. Elwes. London, 1866.

Rask's Icelandic Grammar. By Dasent. London, 1843.

Tauchnitz' Pocket Dictionary of the English and Swedish Languages. Leipsic, 1867.

Welsh and English Dictionary. By W. Owen Pughe, D.C.L. London, 1836.

A GLOSSARY

OF

Furness Words & Phrases

A—of; on; have

> "Though I'd '*a* geen my silver watch
> Just for ya single word."
> *J. S. Bigg.*   Shifting Scenes, p. 172.

Aa—owe   Isl. *aa*   A.S. *áh*

Aamas—alms   A.S.—*ælmesse*

The following quatrain is still remembered by some of the old inhabitants of Furness, as the usual address of beggars soliciting alms :—

> " Pity, pity paamas,
> Pray give us *aamas* ;
> Yan for Peter, two for Paul,
> Three for God 'at meeàd us all." ·

Aan—own   Su. G. *egen*   O.E. *awn*

"Yan o' Slaff sons gat wedt, an' hed a son of his *aan.*"—*Lonsdale Magazine*, vol. 2, p. 90.

Abide—endure   A.S. *abidan*

" Then is better to *abyde* the bur vmbestoundes."
> *Allit. P.* ed. Morris C.1. 7.

Addle—earn "A.S. *ædlean, ædlean*—reward, recompense. *Addle* would therefore signify to give a reward or recompense; to earn in a general sense." —*Morris.*

> " An' sell my daddy's corn an' hay,
> An' *addle* my sixpence ivvery day."
> *Lanc. Ball.* p. 183.

Addle—rotten A.S. *adl* *Addled*-eggs—rotten eggs ; *addle*-heeàd is frequently used as a term of contempt.

Adun—have done, be quiet In Old English, *a* often occurs for *have* in the imperative mood.

> "*A* mercy, madame, on this man here."
> *William of Palerne*, 978.

Afear'd—afraid A.S. *afæred*

> "He mas then vowes, and cryes on Crist,
> For he is *afered* that he sal be peryst."
> *Pricke of Conscience*, ed. Morris, ll. 2942-3.

Aisht—asked

> "Gauan *asshes*, Is it soe ?"—*Avow. K. Art.*, st. xxiv.
> "Then the king *asshed*, Art thou wrothe?"—St. lvii.

Aither—either A.S. *ægther*

> "Chese on *aither* hand,
> Whether the lever ware
> Sinke or stille stand."
> *Sir Tristram*, Hall. Dict.

Alang—along A.S. *andlang* Germ. *entlang*, through the length of

> "Thus past he *alang* many a weary mile,
> In raine, and wet, and in foule mire."
> *The King and a poore Northern Man.*

Ald—old   A.S. *ald*

> " A wyser man may he be talde
> Whether he be yhung or *alde*."
> *Pricke of Conscience*, ll. 213-4.

Ald Lant—stale urine, used for washing clothes

"It wus nowt o'th' warld o God boh arron *owd Lant*."— *Tim Bobbin.*   Tummus and Meary.

Ald-wife hakes—yearly gatherings, or convivial meetings, held about Christmas.   Young and old of both sexes attend, and the evening is spent in tea-drinking, card-playing, and dancing.

Alder—older

> " & ay the ofter, the *alder* they were."
> *Allit. P.* ed. Morris A.l. 620.

Aldest—eldest

"Bott thenne the bolde Baltager, that watz his barn
   aldest,
He watz stalled in his stud, & stabled the rengne."
> *Allit. P.* B.l. 1333-4.

Amackly—in some form or fashion

Amang—among   A.S. *amang*   Isl. *meng-a*, to mix

> "He owt-toke me thare *amang*
> Fra mi faas that war sa strang."
> *Psalm* xvii., *v.* 18., Sp. of E. Eng.

An'—a provincial curtailment of *and*

"It's nobbut this time last year, cum to-morn,
Sen me *an'* Polly walk't to U'ston fair,
Across t' green fields *an'* down t' lang sunny looan,
A gud three mile *an'* mair."
> *J. S. Bigg.*   Shifting Scenes, p. 171.

Angs—the beard of coarse barley

An'ole—and all, also

Apple-Noddy-Day—April fool's day

> " Apple-noddy's past an' gone,
> An' thou's a noddy for thinkin' on."
> *Local Rhyme.*

Argie—dispute   Lat. *arguo*   F. *arguer*

TOURIST : " It's a fine morning."
RUSTIC : " Why, dud I say it wosn't ? dus'ta want
to *argie ?* "

Ark—a large chest used for keeping meal and
flour.   A.S. *arc*, or *earc*, a chest   Su. G. *ark*
Lat. *arca*   Gael. *arc*

Arly—early   A.S. *ærlice*   Moes. Goth. *air*

> " and noght over *arly* to mete at gang,
> ne fer to sit tharat over lang."
> *M. S. Cott. Galba* e. ix., f. 65, Hall. Dict.

Armenac—almanack

Arn—earn   A.S. *earnian*

> " Fore he wyll drynke more on a day,
> Than thou cane lyghtly *arne* in twey."
> *M. S. Ashmole,* Hall. Dict.

Arn'd—errand   A.S. *ærend*

> " And sped hem into Spayne spacli in a while,
> And to the kud King Alphouns kithed here *arnd.*"
> *Will: of Palerne,* 5287.

Arsle—fidget   Belg. *ærselen*, to go backwards

Arval—a funeral

The derivation of this word appears to be from A.S.
erfe, succession to property, and *ealo*, ale ; cf. *bridal*
from the feast named *bride-ale.*   Jamieson says—
"The term has evidently originated from the circum-
stance of an entertainment being given by one who
entered upon the possession of an inheritance."

Arval-bread—bread in the form of cakes, which each guest received at a funeral

Asks—water newts   Gael. *asc*, newt

"*Arskes* may be another form of O.E. *eavroskes*, water-frogs; cf. *lark*, from O.E. *laveroc*."—*Morris*.

> " And *arskes* and other wormes felle,
> That I kan noht in Inglis telle."
> *English Metrical Homilies*, Sp. E. Eng., p. 156.

Ass—ashes Moes. G. *azgo* Isl. *aska* A.S. *ahse*, ashes, a cinder

Assal-tooth—molar tooth   Isl. *jaxl;* so called from being placed near the axis of the jaw

Ass-cat—applied to a dirty child

At—that   O.N. *at*, who, that

> "Those *at* thou gees, at thi yate,
> Quen thou art sette in thi sete."
> *The Anters of Arther at the Tarnewathelan*, st. xiv., l. 10.

At—to A.S. *at*

> " A thowsand yhere and na les,
> Or it com *at* the erth, swa heghe it es."
> *Pricke of Conscience*, ll. 7733-4.

Attercob—a spider's web

Attercop—a spider; literally a poison-cup or poison-head, from A.S. *attor*—poison, and *coppa*—a cup or head

> " Ac wat etestu, that thu ne lighe,
> Bute *attercoppe* and fule vlighe."
> *The Owl and the Nightingale*, Sp. E. Eng., p. 29.

Au—all A.S. *æl*

> "Listeneth now to merlin's saw,
> An' I woll tell to *aw*."
> *Hall. Dict.*

Aukert—awkward A.S. *awoh* O.E. *awk,* wrong, and A.S. *ward,* direction

Back-end—latter part of the year; e.g. " I'se gāèn tà leeàv mè spot (situation) this *back-end.*"

Backston—an iron plate for baking upon Icel. *bakstjarn,* a baking-iron

Badger—a vendor; one who purchases butter, eggs, etc., in country markets, for retailing in large towns. Fr. *bedour* Low Lat. *bladarius,* a corn dealer

Badly—sick, unwell

" I've been rayder *badly* and pain't i' my back."
Wm. Dickinson. Cumb. Ball. p. 528.

Bag-and-Baggage—all a person's goods

Bang—to strike; to beat Sw. *banka,* to knock, pummel

" If that I doe ever meete with your fewd foes,
Ise swear by this staffe that their hide I won *bang.*"
The King and a poor Northerne Man.

Bang—to surpass

" We've *bang'd* the French, aye, out an' out,
An' duin the thing complete."
Miss Gilpin. Cumb. Ballads, p. 62.

Bannock—a cake made of oatmeal, treacle, and a little ginger Gael. *bonnach*

Barfut—bare-foot

"In sumer ge habbeth leave *barfot* gan and sitten."
The Ancren Riwle, Rel. Ant. v. 2, p. 3.

Bariham—a horse collar. Another form of O.E. *hamberwe*. The hames are the two crooked pieces of wood round a horse collar. The stuffing of hay within was called the *hamberwe*, from *hame* and the O.E. *berwe*, a protection. Thus *bariham* means literally the stuffing protecting the hames. See *Hames* in Wedgwood.

Barley-me—to bespeak ; a children's game. The boys call out " Barley !" when they desire a rest or pause in their game. " Fr. *parlez, foi melez*, let us have a truce and blend our faith."—*Jamieson*.

Barn—child A.S. *bearn* Moes. G. *barn*

" And was a big bold *barn*, and breme of his age." *Will: of Palerne*, 18.

" This *barn*, he sed that thou has sene, Is goddes son, wit-outen wene." *Cursor Mundi*, Sp. E. Eng., p. 143.

Barns-lakins—children's playthings A.S.— *lácan*, to play, sport

" In that also that thou sent us a hande-balle and other barne-*laykaynes*."—*M. S. Lincoln*, Hall. Dict.

Barring-out—a school-boys' annual custom of barring the school-room door during the master's absence, when, before admitting him, he had to promise a holiday. The door being secured, two captains were elected ; generally the selection was influenced by the position and circumstances of the parents. Each captain then selected a clerk, who entered the names of the boys as they were called to their respective sides. The school was thus divided into two parties, and the preliminaries were then settled for a game at foot-ball on the holiday which the master was sure to grant. (See Foote-bo.)

Bash—shy, bashful, from *abash*

" I wende no Bretouns walde bee *basschede* for so lyttille."—*Morte Arthure*, l. 2121.

Bass—a species of perch *(Perca Labrax);* a fish found very plentifully in the tarns, lakes, and mill-races of Furness. IOHN RUSSELL in his "Boke of Nurture" says they must be served up with a sauce made of cinnamon :—
" *Baase,* flownders, carpe, cheven, synamome ye ther
to sett."— *The Babee's Book,* p. 174.

Bassen—a basin Fr. *bassin*
"Thagh it be bot a *bassyn,* a bolle, other a scole."
Allit. P. B. l. **1145.**

Bat—a blow A.S. and Gael. *bat,* an imitation of the sound of a blow

Bat—place or position; as "I wos varra weel yesterda, but now I'se at t'ald *bat* again."

Baum—balm Fr. *baume*
" Of herbes and tres, spring *baum* ful gude,
And oyle and wyne for man's fude."
Pricke of Conscience, l. 652.

Be-bo-buntin'—a nursery rhyme
" *Be-bo-buntin',* daddy's gone a huntin',
To catch a rabbit for its skin,
To lap his bonny lile babby in."
Local Rhyme.

" Auld Wulson doz'd as nought had been,
An' clwose by th' hudd sat gruntin';
Wheyle Mary Cairn, to Wulson' bairn
Was singin' *be-bo-buntin'.*"
Mark Lonsdale. Cumb. Ballads, p. 282.

Be—by A.S. *be*
" Sothely they sall joy now *be* in-gettynge of grace,
and in time to come *be* syghte of joy."
Hampole's Prose Treatises, p. 4.

Beetle—a staff with which clothes were formerly beetled or washed. A.S. *bitl, beatan,* to beat.
"Batyledoure or wasshynge betylle."—*Prompt Parv.*

Beetlin'-steeàn—the stone upon which clothes were beetled. A few years ago a large boulder stood by the side of the well at the corner of Well Street, Ulverston, it was then called the "*Beetlin-steeàn.*" Some years before that, the same stone was in the wool market at the foot of Soutergate, and was known as the "Woo'-steeàn.

Beeàn—bone A.S. *ban*

Beeàny-prick—the stickle-back

Beck—a stream Germ. *bach* A.S. *becc* Teut. *beke*

"The brooks, the *becks*, the rills, the rivulets."
Drayton.

"Humpty Dumpty lay in a *beck*
With all his sinews round his neck.
Halliwell's Nursery Rhymes.

Beck-bibby, or Watter Craa—the Dipper, or Water Ouzel. (*Cinclus aquaticus.*)

Beeas—cattle; the north plural form of beast

Beggar-inkle—a coarse narrow tape; the looms by which it was manufactured being so small and compact that a large number could be placed in one room, hence the phrase "as thick as *inkle* weavers;" i.e. particularly intimate.

Be-gock !—a rustic oath. "Thou can't loup that dyke, can t'e?" "Yes, *begock!* I can."

Belder or Beller—to cry A.S. *bellan*, to bellow

" 'Hod thy noise, thoo *bellerin'* coaf, an' hear what I've to say,' says t' fadder, as he gat oot o' patience at Wiff's gowlin'."—*Author of Joe and the Geologist.* Tales and Rhymes, p. 30.

Belkin—belching A.S. *bealcan* O.E. *belke,*
bolke, boke—great. Icel. *bulka*—to swell; e.g. "belkin
full," "a belkin fellow."

Bene's—this is now generally **understood** to
mean the hands.   Nurses say to children—
> "Clap *bene's* for daddy to cum,
> An' bring lile babby a ceäk an' a bun."

The meaning is evidently corrupted from the A.S.
ben—prayer—"clasp your hands and pray," &c.
See *Hall. Dict.*

Bessy—the Yellow Hammer, Yellow Yeörling
(*Emberiza citrinella.*)

Bete—amend; now generally applied to the
fire, as "Bete t' fire."   A.S. *bétan*
> "Quyl I fete sum quat fat thou the fyr *bete.*"
Allit. P. B. l. 627.

> "Wheyle to *beet* on the elden."
John Stagg.   Cumb. Ballads, p. 221.

Bezzler—anything very great

Biddy—a louse   cp. *bott,* a belly-worm ; *boads,*
maggots
> "Bowde, malte-worm."—*Prompt Parv.*

Bigan—begun
> "Cherubin wit chere sa milde,
> *Bigan* to tel him o that child."
Cursor Mundi, Sp. E. Eng., p. 143.

Bigg—barley   Isl. *bygg*   Dan. *byg*
> "An' southy crops o' beans an' *bigg.*"
John Stagg.   Cumb. Ballads, p. 221.

Blaw—blow   A.S. *blæwan*

> "That the beme that *blaw* sal on domsday,
> Sounes in myn eres, that thus says ay
> Ryse yhe that er dede, and come
> Un-to the grete dredful dome."
> *Pricke of Conscience*, ll. 4678-80.

Bléa—livid from cold   Fries. *bla*   O.H. Germ. *blao*   Dan. *blaa*, blue, livid

Bleb—a raised spot, or blister, on the skin —Scotch *bleb*, a drop of water

Bledder—bladder   A.S. *blædre*

> "With a face as fat· as a full *bledder*,
> Blowen bretfull of breth· & as a bagge honged."
> *Pierce the Ploughman's Crede*, ed. Skeat, ll. 222-3.

Blether—nonsense   Sw. *bladra*, to babble   Scotch—*blether, blather, bladder*

Blobber—a bubble   See Bleb.

> "Blobure, blobyr, Burbalium."
> *Prompt. Parv.*

Bob-yak-day—Royal oak day, May 29th

Boggert—a ghost   W. *bwg*, a hobgoblin

Bogie—a small hand-cart of a skeleton construction, used for various purposes

Boon-Ploo'—a custom of very frequent occurrence in Furness, when all the farmers of the neighbourhood on certain occasions make a *boon*, or gift for the day of a man with horses and plough to one of their neighbours.   These are distributed over the farm, and if it is not a large one, most of the land is ploughed before night, which ends in jollity, the recipient finding entertainment for all.

Boose—a stall for a cow   A.S. *bosig*

Borrans—rough craggy places with huge boulders lying about, to which foxes run for security when hard pressed.   A.S. *beorg*, *beorh*, a hill or place of safety.   Germ. *beorgan*, to protect or shelter. Cf. Eng. *borough*, and *burrow*

Bor-tree—the Elder tree

Box—a blow   Dan. *bask*, a sounding blow

"And with his burlyche brande a *box* he hyme reches."—*Morte Arthure*, l. 1111.

Bracken—fern   Sw. *bräken*

"As best, byte on the bent of *braken* & erbes."
Allit. P. B. l. 1675.

Brackin-clock—a small beetle

Brak—broke   Isl. *braak*   A.S. *bræc*

"And he takynge seuene looues, and doyng thankynyes, *brak*, and gaf to his disciples."
The Gospel of St. Mark (Wycliffe's) c. viii., v. 6.

Bran-new—quite new.   "Sist'a, min, I've gitten a par o' *bran-new* clogs on to-day."

Brant—steep; any place difficult of ascent is said to be "varra *brant*."   "Sw. *brant*, steep ; *en brant klippa*, a steep rock."—*Jamieson.*

Brash—rash   A.S. *bꝛæsen*, to rush upon

Brast—burst   A.S. *berstan*   pt. t. *bærst*

"And of the scourges alswa that *brast* his hyde,
That the blode ran doun, on ilk syde."
Pricke of Conscience, A.D. 1340.

Brat—a coarse covering for the dress A.S. *bratt,*
cloak, clout W. *brat,* a clout, pinafore

Bray—to beat, pound Fr. *broyer*

Brek—break Goth. *brikan* Fries. *brekke*

> "Bot at the last thai sal *brek* out
> And destroy many landes obout."
> *Pricke of Conscience,* l. 4465.

Breer—briar A.S. *brér*

> "Red as rose off here colour,
> As bryght as blosme on *brere.*"
> *The Romance of Athelston, Rel. Ant.* v. 2, p. 76.

Brickle—brittle

> "But being fair and *brickle* likest glass did seem."
> *Spencer's Fairy Queen,* B. iv., c. x.

Brig—bridge Su. G. *brygga* · A.S. *bricg*

> "At Trompyngtoun, nat fer fro Cantebrigge,
> Ther goth a brook, and over that a *brigge.*"
> *Ch. Canterbury Tales,* l. 3920.

Brock—badger A.S. *broc*

> "Nea mair i' th' nights thro' woods he leads,
> To treace the wand'ring *brock.*"
> · *Relph.* Cumb. Ball. p. 8.

> "With hart ant hynd, do ant bokke,
> Hare ant foxe, catt ant *brocke.*"
> *A Charter of Edward II., Rel. Ant.,* v. 1, p. 168.

> "And go hunte hardiliche· to hares and to foxes,
> To bores and to *brockes·* that breketh adown mynne
>   hegges."
> *Piers Plowman,* ed. Skeat, Text B, Pass. vi., l. 30.

Brog—a bough   A.S. *bog*   O. E. *bogh*

> "Unnethes he had this word spoken,
> An angel com, a *bogh* was broken."
>> *Cursor Mundi*, Sp. E. Eng., p. 137.

"But ye men-fo'k er sic buzzards, if ye sā a *brog* on t' sand ye wod think it wos t' French.   I've neā patience wi' sic daffy's."—*Siege o' Brou'ton*, p. 6.

Brong—brought, gave

> "Ned Wulson *brong* his lug a whang."
>> *Anderson.*   Cumb. Ball. p. 301.

Brossen—burst   O.H. Germ. *brestan*   A.S. *berstan*

Brown-leemers   See Leemers

Buck't-up—dressed up in the best style. Germ. *butz*   "How fine lile Tommy is to-day!" "Ey! he's parlish grand when he's o' *buck't up* in his Sunday cleeàs."

Built up—to be elevated with false hopes

Bull-jumpings, or beastings—the first milk given after calving, which when boiled forms a custard-like mass, and is then called "Bull-jumpings."

Bullyrag—to use harsh language   "cp. *bully-rook*, a hectoring, boisterous fellow."—*Bailey*.   Sw. *buller*, noise

Bummel-bee—the Humble Bee   Isl. *buml*—resounding

Bung-grog—the washings of spirit casks

But-an-splic—a game played with pins upon a hat, formerly very common in Furness; cf. Jamieson in v Pap—the Bonnet

Butter-shag—a slice of bread and butter

Byre—cow-house   W. *bwr*, an enclosure

Caad—cold   (See Cald)

Caakers—iron rims placed on the under side
of clogs (wooden soled shoes)

Cabbish—cabbage   Fr. *cabouche*

Caff—chaff   A.S. *ceaf*   Du. *kaf*   Flem. *kaf*
> "For als fyre that *caff* son may bryn
> Gold may melt that es lang thar-in."
> *Pricke of Conscience*, ed. Morris, ll. 3148-9.

Caffel—entangle   A.S. *cæfli*   O.E. *kevel*, a gag
Norse *kievla*, to gag   O.N. *kefli*, a peg

Caimt—crooked, bad tempered   W. *cam*—
crooked

Cald—cold   A.S. *cald*   Moes. G. *kalds*   Isl. *kaldr*
> "And I fand Jhesu wery in the way, turment with
> hungre, thrist, and *cald*."
> *Hampole's Prose Treatises*, p. 5.

Calder—colder
> "Thy corse in clot mot *calder* kene."
> *Allit. P. A.* l. 320.

Cample—to retort, contend   Germ. *kampeln*,
to debate, dispute   A. S. *camp*, fight

Capper—to do what another cannot, is to
"Set him a *capper*."
> "Canny auld Cummerlan' *caps* them aw still."
> *Anderson.* Cumb. Ballads, p. 353.

Carpin—speaking Lat. *carpere*

"Ane es ryghte sayeyng and *carpyng* of the wordes."
Dan Jon Gaytryges Sermon, p. 7.

Catty—a game played with a small piece of
pointed wood, a ball, or stone W. *cat*—a small
piece

Chaffs—jaw bones Su. G. *kiaefts* A.S. *ceafl*,
jaw, snout Dan. *kiæft*

"At time when nought but teeth was gaun,
An' aw by th' *chafts* was tether't."
Mark Lonsdale. Cumb. Ballads, p. 239.

Chammerly—urine; chamber-*lye* See Ald
Lant

Chance-barn—an illegitimate child

Chang—noisy talk

Chappel-i-laa—a mode of punishment formerly
resorted to by the boys of Furness, for pulling hazel
nuts before they were ripe. It was conducted in
this manner—The boys dividing themselves into two
rows, laid themselves down with their feet together,
the culprit was then made to run the gauntlet
amongst their legs, when each boy, as opportunity
presented itself, saluted him with a kick.

Chass—to hurry, same as *chase;* originally, to
drive

Chatter-Basket—a name applied to a talkative
child—"Thou's a fair lile *chatter-basket*, that ist'a."

Chepster—the Starling, *(Sturnus vulgaris)*

Chig—to chew

Childer—children   A.S. *cildra, cildru*

> "Thay ere lyke vnto the *childir* that rynnes aftere buttyrflyes."—*Hampole's Prose Treatises*, p. 39.

> "Tharfor maysters som tyme uses the wand,
> That has *childer* to lere undir thair hand."
> *Pricke of Conscience*, ed. Morris, ll. 5880-1.

Chip—to trip a person up; a term used in the wrestling ring.   Sw. D. *kippa*, to totter, be unsteady

Chitter—to talk quickly, chatter

> "As eny swalwe *chiterynge* on a berne."
> *Cant. Tales*, l. 3258.

Chitty—a cat; also the wren commonly called "chitty-wer-wren."

Chock-full—full to the brim, full to choking

> "Charottez *chokkefulle* chargyde with golde."
> *Morte Arthure*, l. 1552.

Chops—jaws

Chow—chew   O.E. *chaw*

> "Deavie, Deavie, corly pow,
> First a bite an' then a *chow*."
> *Old Local Rhyme.*

Churn—a Daffodil; children separate the corolla from the stem bearing the pistil, and working it up and down with a churning motion repeat the following rhyme—

> "*Churn, churn* chop,
> Butter cum ta t' top."

Claa—claw   A.S. *clea*   O.E. *cle*

Claak—to catch hold of, clutch   A.S. *gelæccan* O.E. *cloke*, a claw

Claaty-Molly—a dirty, slovenly woman.   ʻ
Clag and Clarty

Clack—to chatter   F. *claquer*

> "Thar-mid thu *clackest* oft and longe,
> And that is on of thine songe."
> *The Owl and the Nightingale*, Sp. E. Eng., p.

Clag—to adhere Isl. *kleggi* Dan. *klæg*—sti

Clam—to clag up, to dry up.   cf. *clam*
Dan. *klamme*, to cling or cleave together A. S. *cl*
a bandage, also *clay*

> "& thenne *cleme* hit with clay comly with-inne.ʼ
> *Allit Poems*, B. l.

Clanter—to make a noise in walking   (
Clatter)

Clap-breeád—oat-cakes, which were form(
clapped thin with the hands instead of being roll

Clarty—filthy, sticky See Clag

> "That spatel that swa *biclartad* ti leor"—
> That spittle that so defiled or besmeared thy fac
> *O. E. Homilies*, ed. Morris, p.

Clash—to bang a door   Dan. *kladske*, to
Ger. *klatsch*

Clashy—rainy, uncomfortable weather

> "Yence on a *clashy* winter neet,
> Whyte maiz'd wi' loungin' on i' t' nuik."
> *John Stagg.*   Cumb. Ball. p.

Clatter—a noise   Du. *klateren*

Cleg—the gad-fly; *cleg* is but another forn
clag—to stick. This provincial name it has no d(
received on account of the tenacity with whic
adheres to any animal. To "stick like a *cleg*"
common phrase. Dan. *klæg*, sticky N. *klegg*

Clem—to pinch with hunger, to starve. (More generally used in South Lancashire.) A.S. *clæmian*, to pinch Dan. *klemme* O.E. *clam* cf. *clamp*

"Hard is the choice, when the valiant must eat their arms or *clem*."
Ben Jonson.   Ev. Man out of his Hum.

"Booath *clemmin'*, un starvin', un never a fardin',
It 'ud welly drive any mon mad."
Lanc. Ball. p. 217.

"We s' niver, I's insuer us,
Be neeak't, or *clemm'd*, or cāld."
Author of Joe and Geologist.   North Lons. Mag. p. 18.

"Al schal cry for *clemmed*."
Allit P. C. l. 395.

Clew—a ball of worsted is generally called "a woosat *clew*." A.S. *cliwe* O. Du. *klouwe*

Click—catch hold suddenly Frisian *klække*

"He *clekys* owtte Collbrande fulle clenlyche burneschte."—*Morte Arthure*, l. 2123.

Clink—a blow Dan. *klinke*, to rivet

Clit-clat—a term applied to a talkative person

Clish-clash—idle talk; a reduplicate form of Clash—a noise

Clock—a Beetle. This name is applied to beetles generally, as "Bracken-clock," "Black-clock."

Clod—to throw; as "*Clod* it away, thou; it's nasty."

Clog—a wooden soled shoe common through out Lancashire

"My country *clogs* to save my shoon."
Lanc. Ballads, p. 128.

Clot-hee&d—a clod-head, lumpish fellow

Clotter'd—clotted   O.Du. *klotteren*, to c
late.   (See Cludder.)
" *Clottred* clod of seeds."—*Golding.*

Clout—a patch, or piece of cloth   A.
W. *clwt*

> " For ich nabbe *clout* ne lappe,
> Bote lay thou thi fet to my pappe,
> And wite the from the colde."
> *Political, Religious, and Love Poems*, p.

Cludder—to press together, heap tog
connected with *clod*, *clot*, *cloud*

" O' t' poor wimmin i' t' town *cludder'd* roun
'em wi' basens, pots, an' cans of o' kinds."
Invasion o' U' sto

Clunch—a clodhopper

Cob—round, as a "cob-coal"   W. *co*,
ness   W. *cobyn*, a bunch

Cobbin'—when a person's hair is pulle
the company, it is called *cobbin*

> A cobbin', a cobbin, a barley bum,
> Cob them 'at doesn't come ;
> Cob him yance, cob him twice,
> Cob him till he whistles thrice ;
> If he whistles any meear,
> Cob him till his heead's seear !
> *Local Rhyme*

Cockly—unsteady   Germ. *kuglen*   O.N
to roll

Cock-penny—a penny formerly given to
boys in Furness, when they paid their sch
This penny was expected to be staked on th
cock fight, which took place on Shrove Tue

Coddled—embraced, cuddled

"I *coddled* her clwose, an' gave her many a smack."
Ewan Clark. Cumb. Ballads, p. 155.

Cofe-lick—calf-lick, a tuft of hair on the forehead which grows upwards and will not part or lie straight

Coke—the core of any fruit Gael. *caoch*
Dutch *kolk* O.E. *colke*

"Til a rounde appel of a tre,
That even in myddes has a *colke*."
Pricke of Conscience, ll. 6444-5.

Com—came A.S. *com,* pt. t. of *cuman*

"Beestes that now ben‧ mouwen banne the tyme
That evere that cursede Caym‧ *com* vppon eorthe."
Piers Plowman, ed. Skeat, A. Pass. x., ll. 165-6.

Con—a squirrel

"Our young friend dissipated them all [our fears] by telling us that a *con* was only the provincial name for a squirrel."—*Lonsdale Magazine,* vol. 2, p. 124.

Conny—handsome, good-looking ; also used in the sense of quantity, as "There's a *conny* lock on 'em thrang i' t' hay field owerbye." Dan. *kjön,* pretty

Coot—Water Rail "W. *cwta,* bob-tailed, *cwt-iar,* a coot or water-hen."—*Wedgwood.*

'Coord—accord

"Bi good ensaumplis the preestis schuld lere
The vnleerned how thei schulden doo :
If her word & werk *coorde* not in fere."
Hymns to the Virgin and Christ, p. 38.

Coppy-stool—a small wooden stool for children

Corn-craik—the Land Rail   *Craik—crake-* a representation of the sound made by the bird

Corby—the carrion crow; the raven   Fr. *co beau* Ital. *corvo* Lat. *corvus* (Not much used Furness.)

Cote—a cottage, as Lindal Cote, &c.   A.S. *coi* a cottage
> "And there he made a litel *cote*."
>> *Havelok the Dane*, l. 73

Coup—a cart

Cow-grip—the trench in a shippon to receiv the urine   A.S. *grep*
> "And summe leye in dikes slenget,
>   And summe in *gripes*."
>> *Havelok*, l. 1923.

Cow-skarn—cow-dung   Dan. *skarn*, filth

Craa—crow
> *Craa! Craa!* Forness fell
> Gie me a lile apple
> An' I waint tell.
>> *Furness Rhyme.*

Craa-feet—wrinkles about the eyes; the blu flowers of the common Hyacinth

Crack—a chat; in a moment; to boast
> "Come sit thy ways down an' give us thy *crack*."
>> *Dickinson.* Cumb. Ballads, p. 52

Crag—a rock   W. *careg* Gael. *creag*

Creean—to bawl   Sc. *croon*, a long moan

Croft—a small enclosed pasture near a dwelling house A. S. *croft*

> " For t' *croft* was white wid dog-daisies,
>   When Jwohn was teàn away."
> *Author of Joe and Geologist.*   T. and R. p. 50.

Crook—a hook suspended over the fire to hang cooking utensils upon Su. G. *krok* Dan. *krog*

Crouse—brisk, pert   Dan. *kruse*, to curl

> " He is a *crouse* cock."
> *Orth. and Con. of Brit. T.*, p. 28, c. 34.

Crovukt—crushed up or crowded W. *crybwh;* shrunk up.   Ex. " We wer o' *crovukt* in a heeàp."

Cruds—curds W. *crwd*, a round lump

> " And a fewe *cruddes* and craym· and a therf cake."
> *Piers Plowman*, Text A, pass. vii., l. 269.

Crum'lt—fell to pieces, a corruption of crumbled ; Germ. *krümeln*

Cuckoo-spit—a froth found upon plants, enclosing the larva of *cicada spumaria*, an insect allied to the grasshopper

Cuckstool-dub—the pool in which shrews were ducked on the cuckstool ; Butts Beck, Dalton, was formerly known by this name.   My friend Mr. Bolton informs me that in the Court Leet records of Furness, many instances are recorded of this punishment having been inflicted.   Mr. Way, in a note to his edition of the Promptorium Parvulorum, page 107, says—" The earliest mention of this mode of punishing female offenders occurs in the laws of Chester in the time of Edward the Confessor."

" *Kukstole* for flyterys, or schyderys."—*Prompt Parv.*

Cushat—the Ring Dove A.S. *cusceote*

Cushie-cow-lady—Cushie, dear; a term used in addressing a pet. A lady-bird is a favourite insect with children, to which they sing—

> " *Cushie-cow-lady* let down thy milk
> An' thou sall hev a gown of silk."

Cutt'rin' — muttering, whispering; possibly another form of chittering, chattering Du. *koeteren*, to jabber

> " They *cutter'd* on, but varra low."
> *Anderson.*   Cumb. Ball. p. 376.

Dab—very good, as " He's a *dab* hand at it."

Dab—a blow

Dad—father W. *tad*

> " My *dad* an' mam are fast asleep,
> My brother's up an' with the sheep."
> *Jockey to the Fair.*   Old Song.

Daffey—a foolish person A.S. *deaf*, deaf;

> " Thou dotest *daffe*, quath heo· Dulle are thi wittes."
> *Piers Plowman*, Text A, pass. i, l. 129.

Daft—soft, foolish

Dannet—a term of reproach; literally " *do nought*" Dan. *dögenigt*; a worthless fellow

> " Cu' thy ways on thou *dannet*."
> *T' Siege o' Brou'ton*, p. 5.

Darrak—a day's work

> "Thou's meade a bonny *darrack*."
> *Mark Lonsdale.*   Cumb. Ball. p. 276.

Dathit—a mild curse O.Fr. *deshait*, a mishap

> " *Dathit* hwo it hire yeve
> Evere more hwil i live !"
> *Havelok*, 300.

Dazed—starved, cold; bread baked in an insufficiently heated oven is said to be *dazed*; stupefied, IceL *dasdr*, faint; Du. *daesen*, to lose one's wits (see Kilian's Etymologicum).

> "And ay was *dased* in charite."
> *Pricke of Conscience,* l. 6647.

> "I stod as stylle as *dased* quayle."
> *Allit Poems,* A, l. 1084.

Deave—to deafen; to stupify with noise N. *döyva*, to stun, or stupify

> "My minnie does constantly *deave* me."
> *Burns' Poems,* vol. 2, p. 24.

Dedur—to tremble   G. *zittern*   O.E. *diddere*

> "Yette dyntus gerut him to *dedur*,
> He stroke him sadde and sore."
> *Avow. of K. Arth.,* st. xxv., l. 8.

Deead as a dure nail—dead to a certainty; a very common phrase. The nails used for doors are called by the ironmongers "dead nails."

> "And *ded as a dore-nayl·* but the deede folewe."
> *Piers Plowman,* Text A., pass. I, l. 161.

Deet—died

> "He sayd, Jhesu, as thou *deet* on the rode."
> *Sir Amadace,* st. xxxv., l. I.

Deg—to damp, to sprinkle water upon anything. Another form of *dew* Sw. *dagg* Dan. *dug*

Dett—debt

> "The *dette* of payn may be qwitte son."
> *Pricke of Conscience,* l. 3617.

Deuce—the devil ; Du. and Fr. *deus*, the deuce ! Armor. *teuz*, a demon. For the derivation of this word "lexicographers have sent us to the *Dusii* of S. Augustine, the *Dues* of the Gothic nations, the *Teus* of the Armoricans, &c., &c. !! Thomson says, 'all these words, like dæmon, seem to have been once used in a *good sense ;*' and in fact are all corruptions of the same root."

Note by Sir F. Madden to *Havelok.*

Lat. *Deus*, old Teutonic *Tiw* or *Teus*, all mean God : and secondarily, the devil.

"*Deus !* lemman ! hwat may this be ?"
Havelok, l. 1312.

" *Deuce* tek the clock ! click-clackin sae."
Anderson. Cumb. Ball. p. 308.

Dibs—money ; as, "Down wi' thy *dibs*, then."
See Gregor's " Dialect of Banffshire."

Diddle-daddlin—dawdling about. See Gregor's " Dialect of Banffshire."

Dilly-dallying—procrastinating, putting things off; a reduplication of *dally*, to lose time

" There ne'er comes luck of *dilly-dallying* wark."
Ewan Clark. Cumb. Ball. p. 162.

Ding—to strike   Icel. *dengia* Sw. *dänga*

" Thus sall thai *dyng* on them ever-mare,
With gret glowand hamers and nane spare."
Pricke of Conscience, l. 7031.

Dinnel—to tingle

Divel's-bow-an'-arrow

" The spink and the sparrow,
Are the *divel's-bow-an'-arrow.*"
Nursery Rhyme.

Divel's snuff-box—the common puff-ball, a fungus *(Lycoperdon.)*

Dobby—a ghost

"Ghosts ! eigh me lad, we've plenty on 'em i' Forness, but we'd anudder neeam for 'em ; we ol'as co'd 'em *dobbies* or freet'nins."—*Lebby Beck Dobby*, p. 3.

Dockin—the common dock, popularly considered to be a certain cure for the sting of a nettle, if, when rubbed over the wound the words "dockin in, nettle out" be repeated three times.

"Nettle in, dock out" occurs in *Chaucer;* Troilus, bk. iv. l. 461.

Dodder—to shake ; *totter*, quiver ; as " Doddering grass."

Doff—undress, literally do off

"And thou my concelle doo, thow *doffe* of thy clothes."
Morte Arthure, l. 1023.

"Knowing manners, what I *doff'd* my hat to aw strangers."—*Anderson.* Cumb. Ball. p. 368.

Dog—when a portion only of a rainbow can be seen it is called a *dog.* The following is a proverbial saying in Furness—

> " A rainbow in the morning
> Is the shepherd's warning ;
> A *dog* in the night
> Is the sailor's delight."

That is—a rainbow seen in the morning betokens a wet day ; but if part of one is seen in the evening, it is the precursor of fine weather."—cf. *Dog* Gregor's " Dialect of Banffshire."

Doit—a small share, as, "Give me my *doit;*" a small object, as, "What a *doit!*" According to Jamieson, a *doit* was a small coin formerly current, about one-twelfth of a penny in value. Fr. *doigt* Lat. *digitus*, a finger—*doit* would then be as much as a finger would cover.

Don—to put on clothes, literally do on

> "That Grim bad Leve bringen lict,
> For to *don* on his clothes."
> > *Havelok the Dane*, l. 576.

> "When th' order comes to us
> To doff these owd clooas
> There'll surely be new uns to *don*."
> > *Waugh's Lancashire Songs*, p. 40.

> "Auld England's gown's worn till a tatter,
> An' they'll nit new *don* her I fear."
> > *Miss Blamire.* Cumb. Ball. p. 52.

Donk—moist, damp Dan. D. *dönke*, to make damp Cf. Du. *donker*, dark O.E. *dank*

> "Deowes *donketh* the dounes."
> > *Lyrical Poems.* Sp. E. Eng. p. 108.

Douk—to duck Dan. *dukke*, to dive

Douker—i.e. the *ducker*, a sea bird (*Colymbus auritus.*)

Douse—to throw water upon any person

Dowly—lonely, dull Connected with Su. Goth. *daaleg*, weak ; Dan. *daarlig*, foolish

> "But loave ! it is a *dowly* pleace when winter neeghts
> growe lang."
> *Author of Joe and the Geologist.* T. and R. p. 63.

Down-fo—a fall of rain, hail, or snow

> "But a sawp o' *downfo*' ud do a seet o' good just
> neeaw."—*Waugh*. Sketches of Lanc. Life, p. 199.

Dow—good   Germ. *taugen,* to be fit for, avail
A.S. *dugan,* to profit   Dan. *due,* to be good or fit
for anything

> "For dancin' he was nought at *dow,*
> But a prime han' for a drinker."
>> *Mark Lonsdale.*   Cumb. Ball. p. 213.

> "In aw her flegmagaries donn'd
> What is she?—nought at *dow.*"
>> *Anderson.* Ibid p. 279.

Draff—malt grains after brewing   Icel. *draf*

> "And I lye as a *draf*-sak in my bed."
>> *Cant. Tales.* l. 4240.

Dree—slow, tedious, as "I gat it done at last,
but it wos a varra *dree* job."   Dan. *dröi,* heavy,
tedious

Dub—a pool; literally a *dip* or *deep* place

Duds—ragged clothes   Gael. *dud,* rags

Dummel-heeàd—a blockhead   Cf. *dummy*

Dure—door   A.S. *duru*

Dwinnal—dwindle   A.S. *dwinan*

Eaa—the channel of a river on the sands
A.S. *eá,* a stream.   Ex. "How's t' *eaa?*"—how is
the channel, is it good crossing?

Earls—an earnest penny   Gael. *iarlus*

Eggin—inciting   O.N. *eggia*   A.S. *eggian*

> "The drede of God es that we turne noghte agayne
> till oure syne thurghe any ill *eggyng.*"
>> *Hamp. Prose Treat.* p. 12.

> "Bot thurgh the *eggyng* of Eve he ete of an apple."
>> *Allit. P. B.* l. 241.

Eigh—yes

"Hoo cou'd naw opp'n her meawth t' sey *eigh* or now (no) boh simpert an sed *iss.*"—*Tim Bobbin.*

Eilet-hooals—holes through which a band passes

"*Oylet,* made yn a clothe, for sperynge."
Prompt. Parv.

Elba—elbow

Elba-greace—to work hard upon anything is said to "give it elba greace."

Eldin—fuel A.S. *æld,* fire Su. G. and Sw. *eld*

"*Eldynge,* or fowayle. *Focale.*"—*Prompt. Parv.*

"While to beet on the *elden.*"
John Stagg. Cumb. Ball. p. 221.

Eller-tree—Alder-tree (*Alnus glutinosa*)

"In the north the *alder* is called an *eller,* whence several names of places, as Ellerbeck, Ellerburn, &c. in Yorkshire, are derived. A.S. alr, *alnus.* 'An ellyrtre, *alnus; alnetum est locus ubi crescunt.*'—CATH. ANG."—*Prompt. Parv.*

Erchin—hedge-hog Lat. *ericius* Cf. Fr. *héris-*
ser, to bristle. "An vrchone, *ericius, erinacius.*" CATH. ANG. "Urchone, *herisson.* Irchen, a lytell beest full of prickes, *herison.*" PALSG. In Italian "*Riccio,* an vrchin or hedgehog." FLORIO. Horman says that "Yrchyns or hedgehoggis be full of sharpe pryckillys; porpyns have longer pryckillys than yrchyns." According to Sir John Maundevile, in the Isles of Prester John's dominions "there ben Urchounes als grete as wylde swyn."
Prompt. Parv. p. 512.

Ev'n-doun—straight down; very great, as
"An *ev'n-doun sham.*"

Ew-tree—Yew-tree

"*V tree.*"—*Prompt Parv.*

Ex—ask

Faat—fault   Fr. *faute*

Fadder—father   A.S. *fader*

"The persoun of the town hir *fader* was."—*Chaucer.*

Faffment—nonsense, balderdash

Fairin'—a treat given by the country lads to their sweethearts on the Fair-day

Fairy-pipes—tobacco pipes, with very small and peculiar shaped bowls, frequently turned up with the plough.   These pipes are of various dates, generally from the reign of Elizabeth to James II.

Fald—a yard, a fold   A.S. *fald*

"Under a trouthe in haly kirkes *falde.*"
Pricke of Conscience, l. 4640.

Fand—found   *pt. t.*

"I rane the wanntonnes of flesch and I *fand* noghte Jhesu.   I satt in companyes of worldly myrthe and I *fand* noghte Jhesu.   In all thire I soghte Jhesu bot I *fand* hym noghte."—*Hamp. Prose Treat.* p. 4.

Fan-teckl'd—freckled, having small spots on the face

Farish-on—in liquor, "half seas over"

Fash—trouble, disturbance   Fr. *fâcher*

"What, mun I still be *fash'd* wi' stragglin' sheep?"
Relph.   Cumb. Ball. p. 18.

Feckless—gainless, a bungler   Dan. *jeg fik*, I acquired, gained

> "Indeed, there was some *feckless* fwok,
> That luik'd to be owre nice,
> That nobbet nibblin' pyk't an' eat,
> Just like as monie mice."
> *John Stagg.*   Cumb. Ball. p. 200.

Feeàg—a flatterer   A.S. *fægnian*, to flatter

This appears to be another form of the old Norfolk word, "*Fagyn* or *flateryn*."
See *Prompt Parv.* NOTE p. 146.

Fel-faa—Field-fare   *(Turdus pilaris)*

Fell—a skin   A.S. and Germ. *fell*   Ex. "*feil-monger*," a dealer in skins

Fell—a mountain (the same word as Eng. *field)*

> "Thow sall foonde to the *felle*, and forraye the mountes."—*Morte Arthure*, l. 2489.
>
> London for riches, Preston for pride,
> Kendal for poverty on the *fell-side*.
> *Local Rhyme.*

Fellon—a sore

"*Furunculus*, a soore called a *felon ;* also a soore callid a cattes hear, whiche happeneth on a man's fynger.   ELYOT."—*Prompt. Parv.*

Fellon-wood—the plant Bitter-Sweet   *(Solanum Dulcamara.)*

Fendin'—striving, seeking, as "*Fendin'* fer a leevin'."   A.S. *fandian*, to seek

Fettle—to make ready, set right   N. *fitla*

"When hit watz *fettled* & forged & to the fulle graythed."
Allit. P. B. l. 343.

"Come, we mun *fettle* up oursells,
It's time we sud be donnin'."
John Stagg.   Cumb. Ball. p. 198.

Fic-fac—the tendonous parts of meat

Fidge—an uneasy person, a fidget

" Fidgin' fain."—*Burns.*

Firm as Hodge wife—Hodge's wife is said to
have been confirmed (by the Bishop) several times,
and the phrase is now applied to anything very firm
or secure

Flaach—to wheedle   G. *flehen*, to beseech
O. E. *fleech*

Flang— threw, flung

Flannin—flannel

Flap—a stroke   Du. *flap*

" And thane Alexander sett hym up in his bedd,
and gaffe hymselfe a grete *flappe* on the cheke."
M. S. Lincoln, A. i. 27, f. 48.   (Hall.)

Flay—to frighten   O.N. *flæja*, to flee

" Na vonder es if the devels com than
In the ende obout a synful man,
For to *flay* hym and tempte and pyn."
Pricke of Conscience, l. 2242.

" Divent be *flait* on them, lad Tom,
But let's cower doon i' this dyke back."
John Stagg.   Cumb. Ball. p. 218.

Fleak—a flatterer (see Flaach) ; a flook o₁ plaice   A.S. *floc*, a flat fish

> "fflatt mowthede as a *fluke*, with fleryande lyppys."
> *Morte Arthure*, l. 1088

Flee-ma-geary—anything very showy or dashing

Fleet t' milk—to skim the milk, take off th₁ cream.   "A.S. *flotan*, to float ; O.N. *flót*, the ac of floating ; the grease swimming on the surfac of broth."—Morris' Gloss. to *Allit. P.*

"To fleet, or skim the cream, is a verb still com monly used in East Anglia, and the utensil whic serves for the purpose is termed a *fleeting*-dish.   ' *flete* mylke, take away the creame that lyeth abov it when it hath rested.'   PALSG.   ' *Esburrer*, to *fla* the creame potte ; *laict* esburré, *fleeted* milke ; *maign* *fleeted* milke or whaye.'—Hollybands' *Treasur* "Escremé, *fleeted*, as milke, uncreamed."   COT₁ A.S. *flet, flos lactis*."—Way in *Prompt. Parv.*

Fleish—flesh

> "forsothe the spirit is redy, but the *fleisch* syk."
> *Gospel of Mark*, c. xiv, v. 38.   (Wycliffe's.

Flick—a side of bacon, flitch

> "Befe and moton wylle serve wele enow ;
> And for to seche so ferre a lytill bakon *flyk*."
> *Rel. Ant.* v. 2, p. 2₁

Flipe—the brim of a hat   Icel. *flipa*   Dan. *fli₁* a flap

Flit—to remove   Dan. *flytte*

Flite—to scold   A.S. *flitan*

> "*Flytin*, or chydin—CONTENDO."—*Prompt Parv*

> "Slynge awey these scorners, he seith· with he₁
> shrewid *fliting*."—*Piers Plowman*, Pass. viii. l. 125.

Flosh—water, or a watery place, hence the "*Flosh* meadows" in several parts of Furness. Germ. *fluss*, a flood

Floo's—a sluice   (See Flosh)

Fluet—a blow with the back of the hand

> "Fetch'd him a *fluet* under t' lug,
> An' sae began their battle."
> > *John Stagg.*   Cumb. Ball. p. 203.

Fluz'd—turned up at the edges

Fo—fall, as "Mind that barn dusn't *fo* off t' chair."

Fodder—food for cattle

> "*Foddur*, bestys mete, or forage."—*Prompt. Parv.*
> "for thenne mot ha thenchen of the cuwes *foddre.*"
> > *Rel. Ant.* v. 2, p. 3.

Fog—the aftermath   W. *ffwgws*, dry leaves

> "He fares forth on alle foure, *fogge* watz his mete,
> & ete ay as a horce when erbes were fallen."
> > *Allit. P.* B. ll. 1683-4.

Fo'in owt—quarrelling

Foisty—spoken of a musty smell or taste; mouldy bread is called *foisty*, i.e. fusty

Foomert—the common marten *(martes foina)* sometimes confounded with the pole-cat *(mustela putorius.)* (See *Foumart* in Wedgwood and quot. to Frith.)

Fo'n—fallen

Foor—a furrow made by the plough

Foor-brest—right in front

"On frounte in the *fore-breste*, the flour of his knyghtez."
Morte Arthure, l. 1990.

**Forrat—forward, early, as "a varra *forrat*
tung ;" "*forrat* taties."**

For-elders—forefathers

"Sum on 'em hes left barns behint 'em 'at m'appen
wadn't like to see the'r *for-elders* neeàms mix't up wi'
sic a bit o' Forness 'Linch laa.'"
T' Invasion o' U'ston, p. 7.

**For-end—the beginning, as "t' *for-end* o' t'
yeer ;" the front part of anything**

**Forness—the district of Furness, *fer-nese*, the
further promontory ; a furnace**

"As a *fornes* ful of flot that vpon fyr boyles."
Allit P. B. l. 1011.

Fornenst—opposite

**Forset—to waylay   A.S. *forsettan*, to stop,
delay**

"'At ola's *foorsett* me i't' lonnings aboot
An' beath want to sweetheart me—Jwohnny git oot !"
Author of "Joe and the Geologist." Cumb. Ball. p. 428.

Fra—from   O.N. *frá*

"Aristotill sais that the bees are feghtande agaynes
hym that will draw thaire hony *fra* thaym."
Relig. Pieces, p. 8.

Fratchin'—quarrelling

"Twea girnin' gibbies in a neuk
    Sat *fratchin'* yen anudder,
An' nowte wad sarra them but they
    Wad hev a match together."
John Stagg.   Cumb. Ball. p. 204.

Frap—a blow   Fr. *frapper*

"And *frappez* faste at hys face fersely ther-aftyr."
Morte Arthure, l. 1115.

Freàt—to fret or grieve

Freet—a fright

Fridge—to rub, produce friction   Lat. *fricare*

Frith—a wood   W. *ffridd*

"The fox & the folmarde to the *fryth* wyndez."
Allit P. B. l. 534.

Frosk—a frog   A.S. *frosc*

My friend Mr. Bolton tells me this term was only employed at Urswick, in Low Furness, with regard to those frogs which were of a very light yellow colour.

"Germ. *frosch*, Dan. *frosk*, a frog."   "*Rana*, a froske, or frogge ORTUS."   "A froske, *agredula rana*."—*Way* in Prompt. Parv.

"As the felle of a *froske*"—as the skin of a frog.
Morte Arthure, l. 1081.

Frunt—to affront   Fr. *affronter*

Fuffy—woolly, spongy   Dan. *fug*, flue, fluff

Full-but—right in front

"*ffulle-butt* in the frounte he flysches hyme evene."
Morte Arthure, l. 2769.

Fund—found, *pp.*

"& is *funde* ful few of hit fayth dedes."
Allit P. B. l. 1735.

Fuz-bo—a fungus *(Lycoperdon)*   Du. *voos*, spungy

Ga—go   Icel. *ga*

" Thane the prioure said till hym, *gaa* and wrytte thy synnes."   DE IN-PERFECTA CONTRICIONE.
Hamp. Prose Treats. p. 7.

Gaain'-at-Bruk—going to make cheese ; break the milk

Gaby—a soft person ; literally a *gaping* person

Gaddin'—going about ; a *gaddin'* woman is one that runs about to her neighbours' houses instead of remaining at home

Gaily—very

" Ya het foorneun when we war o' *gaily* thrang."
Author of "Joe and the Geologist."   T. and R. p. 1.

Gainest—the readiest, nearest   Sw. *gen*, near

" And graythes to Glasschenberye the gate at the *gayneste*."—*Morte Arthure*, l. 4309.

Gakin'—staring about

Galevantin—pleasuring, jaunting

Gamashes—leggings

" Gramashes, gaiters reaching to the knees.   A kind of stockings worn instead of boots.   Fr. *gamaches*."—*Jamieson*.   (See *Gamashes* in Wedgwood.)

Gammerstang—a tall awkward woman   O.E. *gammer*, an old woman   Dan. *stang*, a pole.

" I' the loft they were rwoaring an' dancing ;
Big Nancy, the greet *gammerstang*,
Went up an' doon t' fluir lyke a hay-stack,
An' fain wad hev coddled Ned Strang."
The Raffles Merry Neet.   Cumb. Ball. p. 533.

Gang—to go   A.S. *gangan*   O.N. *ganga*

"The Lawyer he is sike a crafty elfe,
A will make a foole of twenty such as me,
And if that I sald *gang* hang mysel,
Ise trow, he and I sud neere agree."
The King and a Poore Northerne Man.

Ganny—grandmother

Gap—an opening   Sw. *gap*

"That no man may fynd path or *gap*,
The world is turnyd to another shap."
Rel. Ant. v. 2, p. 29.

Garn—yarn   Dan. *garn*

Gauk-handed—left handed   Fr. *gauche*

Gaukie—awkward   Fr. *gauche*

Gauster—a horse laugh—"a girt *gausterin* thing"

Geàl—to smart or itch with cold   Fr. *geler*, to freeze.   Ex. "Mi fingers fair *geàl* again wi' cald."

"This auld-far'd chronicle could tell
Things that yen's varra lugs wad *geale*."
John Stagg.   Cumb. Ball. p. 222.

Geàn—gone   O.E. *gan*, gone

Gear—any kind of property; clothing   A.S. *gearwa*

"A wain thai had thair *gere* wit-in."
Cursor Mundi, Sp. E. Eng. p. 135.

"That we gon gay in oure *gere*, that grace he vus sende."
Allit P. B. l. 1811.

Geàt—a way or path   Su. G. *gata*   O.N. *gata,*
a path
  "Of whase *gate* men may na trace fynd."
                    Pricke of Conscience, l. 7076.

  "It's olez summer where th' heart's content,
    Tho' wintry winds may blow ;
  An' theer's never a *gate* 'at's so kind to th' fuut,
    As th' *gate* one likes to go."
                    Waugh's Lanc. Songs, p. 50.

Geàvlock—an iron crowbar   A.S. *gafeloc,* a
javelin   W. *gaflach*

Gebby—a hooked stick

Gers—grass   A.S. *gers, gærs*
  "And syr Gawayne the gude in his gaye armes
  Umbegrippede the *gerse,* and one grouffe fallene."
                    Morte Arthure, ll. 3944-5.

Gezlins—goslings

Giglin—laughing—ex. "a girt *giglin* lass"
O. Du. *gickelen*

Gill—a ravine   Icel. *gil,* a gap in a mountain

Gimmer—a two year old sheep   Su. G. *gimmer*

Gin—a machine for drawing ore

Girdle—a plate of iron for baking upon
W. *greidyll*   Eng. *grid-iron*
  "Aunt Ester spoil'd the *gurdle* ceakes."
                    Anderson. Cumb. Ball. p. 301.

Girn—to grin   Sw. *grina*, to grin

> "Jim and George were two great lords,
> They fought all in a churn ;
> And when that Jim got George by the nose,
> Then George began to *girn*."
> > *Hall. Nursery Rhymes*, p. 12.

Girsly—gristly

Gizzen—gizzard

Giversum—avaricious   A.S. *gifer*, greedy

Gladder—more glad

> "Who that drynketh wele, mych is he the *gladder*,
> Who that drynketh to moch, more is he the madder."
> > *Rel. Ant.* v. 2, p. 288.

Glent—to slip aside   W. *ysglent*, a slide

> "Bot ffloridas with a swerde, as he by *glenttys*,
> Alle the flesche of the flanke he flappes in sondyre."
> > *Morte Arthure*, l. 2781.

Gliff—a glimpse

> "Here, here it was (a wae light on the pleace,)
> That first I gat a *gliff* o' Betty's feace."
> > *Relph.*   Cumb. Ball. p. 16.

Glime—to look askance, glance aside

> "Heedless I *glym'd*, nor could my een command."
> > *Relph.*   Cumb. Ball. p. 16.

Glisk—to shine, sparkle, glisten   A.S. *glisnian*
O.N. *glyssa*

Gloppen—to alarm, astonished   O.N. *glàpa*, to stare

"Thow wenys to *glopyne* me with thy gret wordez."
Morte Arthure, l. 2580.

"Then bounce goos hur heart, an' hoo were so *gloppen*,
That out o' th' winder hoo'd like for to loppen."
Warrikin Fair, A.D. 1548.   Lanc. Ball. p. 69.

"Quen Jhesus sagh tham *glopnid* be,
He lighted of his moder kne."
Cursor Mundi, Sp. E. Eng. p. 134.

Gloppers—blinders for a horse   O.N. *glàpa*, to stare

Glour—to stare   Du. *gloren*, to glitter

"Theire's braw lads in Earnslaw, Marion,
Quha gape and *glowr* wi' their ee."
Percy's Rel. p. 213.

Glumpin—sulking

Gob—mouth   Gael. *gob*   Dan. *gab*   O.E. *gobet*, a mouthful

The following brief dialogue is said to have occurred in Cheshire :—
DOCTOR : "Put out your tongue, my boy."
BOY : "Au dunna whot yo meon."
MOTHER : "Yo shud speik Inglish, doctor !—oppen thi *gob*, Tum lad, an' pull aat thi loliker."

"Because he knew reet weel sud he
Set up his *gob*, directly she
Would kick up hell's delight i' t' house,
Which meade him mum as onie mouse."
John Stagg.   Cumb. Ball. p. 224.

Goff—a fool   Fr. *goffe*

Goke—a fool   Sw. *gäck*

"I ga gowlende a-bowte· al so dos a *goke*."
Rel. Ant. v. 1, p. 291.

Gollin—the Marsh Marigold   Scotch *gowan*

Gome—understanding   Moes. G. *gaumjan*, to perceive

Gomeless—thoughtless, ex. "a girt *gomeless* thing"

Gomeral—a stupid fellow   Icel. *gambra*, to boast

"T' girt *gomerals* hed tacken some brogs on t' sand for t' French masts."—*Siege o' Brou'ton*, p. 7.

Goose-fleish—the skin pimpled from cold

Goul—to howl, yell   O.N. *gola*, to yell

"For unnethes es a child born fully
That it ne bygynnes to *goule* and cry."
Pricke of Conscience, l. 476.

Gradely—real, decent, truly, well, right, hand-somely, orderly. This is a word of almost universal application, and in the way of approval it has many shades of meaning which will perhaps be best under-stood from the quotations. "Just th' same as a *gradely* Christian."—*Waugh*. Tufts of Heather, p. 44. "Iv yo'n a *gradely* greight skip."—Ibid, p. 35. "Dray up to th' hob, an warm yo, for yo look'n *gradely* parisht."—*Waugh*. Sketches of Lanc. Life, p. 20. "Aw'll find yo some *gradely* good stuff."—Ibid. p. 21. "Neaw, ta care yo coan th' next time yo com'n thiz gate, an' wi'n have a *gradely* do."—Ibid, p. 55. In one of our oldest Lancashire romances, "The avowynge of King Arther, Sir Gawan, &c.," stanza lxii., the same word appears in the form of *grathely* :—"With gode wille *grathely* hom gete." In an old Lancashire poem of the 14th century, called by Mr. R. Morris, "The Pearl," it appears as follows—"In sample

he can ful *graythely* gesse."—*Allit P. A.* l. 498.
O.N. *greitha*, to unfold, set right ; A. S. *ge-rædian*,
to make ready ; O.E. *graithe*, to prepare. The
Du. *gereed*, ready, G. *bereit*, ready, shew that *g* is
merely a prefix, and *gradely* is only another form of
readily, with the meaning *exactly, completely*, &c.

Grapplin—a common mode of catching trout,
by wading in the becks and grappling the fish under
stones or in holes by the side of the brook. "Grop-
ing for trout" occurs in *Meas. for Meas.* I. 2.

Greeàn—to groan   O.E. *grane*

Greavin—delving   A.S. *grafan*, to dig, grave
"Gravyn, or grubbyn yn the erth.   FODIO."
Prompt. Parv.

Grece—the inclined way to a barn or granary,
when built over a shippon or stable   Fr. *gré*, a step.
" *Gradus*, a grece, a steppe ; *scamnum*, a steppe or
grice, whereby a manne gothe vppe into a hygh bedde.
Grece to go up at, or a stayre, *degré*."
Way in Prompt. Parv.

Green-hew—an old manorial rent, still paid
in the parish of Dalton, for liberty to cut pea-sticks,
etc., in certain woods

Grey-George—an earthenware bottle.   Some
dialects use *brown-George*

Grime—to soil, blacken   Norse *grima*, a spot
"To spotty, ho is of body to *grym*."
Allit P. A. l. 1069.

Grogram—a coarse stuff for dresses   Fr. *gros-
grain*, coarse grain
" Let other lasses shine in silken gowns,
An' fix fause hair upo' their cockin' crowns,
Sec fashions I'll ne'er follow while I'se whick,
Lang as plain *grogram* and thur locks please Dick.
Ewan Clark. Cumb. Ball. p. 161.

Grund—the earth

> "That al thair idels, in a stund,
> Grovelings fel into the grund."
>> *Cursor Mundi*, Sp. E. Eng. p. 138.

Grunstan,—grindstone

Haffel—to hesitate in speaking

Hagworm—the common snake; literally, *hedge-worm*

Haister—a hastener, Dutch oven

> "*Hastlere* that rostythe mete.   ASSATOR, ASSARIUS."
>> *Prompt. Parv.*

Hack—pickaxe   Fr. *hacher*, to hack

> "For-wroght wit his *hak* and spad,
> Of himself he wex al sad."
>> *Cursor Mundi*, Sp. E. Eng. p. 140.

> April wi' his *hack* an' bill,
> Sets a flow'r on iv'ry hill.
>> *Local Rhyme.*

Hald—hold · A.S. *haldan*

> "And put away fulle mony of your men,
> And *hald* butte on, quere ye *hald* ten."
>> *Sir Amadace*, st. i, l. 10-11.

Ham-sam—confusion, untidy

Hank—a loop of yarn or thread

"Bishop Kennett gives—'a *hànk* of yarn or thread, when it comes off the reel, and is tied in the middle, or twisted.' Perhaps from Sax. *hangan*, to tie or twist; but it comes much nearer to the Isl. *haunk*."
>> *Way* in Prompt Parv. p. 238.

Hankle—to twist, entangle   (See Hank)

"Yes, said the landlord, the ground is rough, and
without care, you may get *hankled* among the bushes."
Lonsdale Magazine, v. 2, p. 124.

Hangment—an expletive, as "What the *hangment* is ta du'in?"

"What the *hangment* has ta sent it us for?"
Waugh's Besom Ben.

Hansel—to be the first purchaser   A.S. *hand-
selen*, a giving into the hands

Hansh—to snap the jaws   O.Fr. *hancher*

Hap—to cover; another form of *lap*, *wlap*,
or *whap*

"Lappyn, or whappyn yn clothys; happyn togedyr,
wrap togedyr."—*Prompt. Parv.*

    "Come, Matty, come, and cool my yed
    Aw'm finished, to my thinkin';
    Hoo *happed* him nicely up, an' said,
    'Thae's brought it on wi' drinkin'.'"
Waugh's Lanc. Songs, p. 32.

Hask—harsh, keen, dry.   A keen frosty wind
is said to be "varra *hask*"   Sw. *härsk*

Haver-breeàd — oat bread   G. *hafer*, oats

"*Haver*, an old term for oats."—*Jamieson.*

"O whar gat ye that *haver*-meal bannock?"
Jamieson's Dict.

Haw-buck—a country clown

Heck—a half door or hatch; a gate   Du. *hek*, a gate

> " Hec, hek, or hetche, or a dore.   ANTICA."
> *Prompt. Parv.*

> " And sum brozt gret harwos,
> Ther husbandes hom to fetch,
> ·Sum on dores, and sum on *hech*."
> *Tourn. Tott.*   Percy's Rel. p. 95.

Hee—high

Heeàd-wark—the head-ache

"The following occurs among several prescriptions for the *hede warke*:—Make lie of verveyn, or of betayne, or of wormode, and there with wasshe thln hed thryse in the weke."—*Prompt. Parv.*

Heft—haft   G. *heft*

Hefter—very large

Helter-skelter—in confusion

> " Back *helter-skelter*, panic struck,
> T'wards heame they kevell'd, yen an' a'."
> *John Stagg.*   Cumb. Ball. p. 218.

Helve—a handle or shaft, as a hammer *helve*

Hempland—a small piece of land set apart for growing Flax for family use. It was spun by members of the family, and woven by the custom weaver. Although the practice has fallen into desuetude, the patches of land still retain the name.

Heriot—a death fine
"This primarily signified the tribute given to the lord of a manor for his better preparation for war, but came at length to denote the *best aucht*, or beast of whatever kind, which a tenant died possessed of."— *Jamieson.*   "A tribute given to the lord of a manor

for his better preparation toward the war, now the best chattle that a tenant hath at death due to the lord by custom or service."—*Coles.*   A.S. *here-geatu*, a warlike provision

Hesp—a clasp or hook   Germ. *häspe*   O.N. *hespa*

Hezal-oil—a thrashing with a hazel wand

Hidin'—a flogging

Hilloky—hilly

Hind—a ploughman, or an upper servant placed in charge of a farm   A.S. *hina*, a servant

> "Our hoste him axed, what man art thou?
> Sir, (quod he,) I am an *hine;*
> For I am wont to go to the plow,
> And earne my meate er that I dine."
> *Notes to Piers Plow. Crede,* p. 45.

Hindersum—obstructive

Hindermast—the last   Moes. G. *hindumists*

Hippin—a napkin

Hitty-missy—hit it or not; literally, hit I or miss I ; or, hit he or miss he ; like *willy-nilly*

Hives—water blebs on the skin

Hoble-de-hoy—between a youth and a man "Girt *hoble-de-hoy*, nader man ner boy."

Ho'd—hold   "Seaz *hod*, min ! can't t'e !" take hold

Hog'us—a house or hutch on the fells for sheep A *hog* is a young sheep ; see *Hall.*

Hoit—a clumsy person   Icel. *hauta*, to flutter about

Hollin—the Holly-tree

"Bot in his on honde he had a *holyn* bobbe
That is grattest in grene, when greuez ar bare."
        Sir Gaw. and Gr. Knt.   Sp. E. Eng. p. 227.

Honish't—wearied, tired out

"Bote *honesschen* him as an hound· and hoten him
go thennes."—*Piers Plowman*, Text A. Pass. xi. l. 48.

Horse-nop—the knap-weed *(Centaurea nigra)*

Horse-stang—the dragon-fly

Howk—to pull up by the roots

Howmer—to shade   Fr. *ombre*   Lat. *umbra*

Huff—rage ; to offend

"Gif thow *hufe* alle the daye, thou bees noght
delyverde."—*Morte Arthure*, l. 1688.

Hull—a covering ; potatoes covered for the
winter are *hulled.*· Cp. pig-*hull* A.S. *helan*, to cover

Hulk—a lazy fellow

Hullet—the owl ; so called from its peculiar
howling cry   Sc. *howlet*

"Foke used tà say it wod screeam like a *hullet*."
        Lebby Beck Dobby, p. 4.

Hully-butterflee—properly the Tiger moth
(Arctia caja), but the term is' indiscriminately applied to any of the heavy bodied night-flying moths

Hurkle—to stoop or squat   Du. *hurken*
O.N. *hurka*

"Then come ther in a litill brid into his arme fleghe,
And ther *hurkils* and hydis as sche were hande tame."
Morris's Gloss. to Allit. P. p. 162

Hysta—make haste   Sw. *hasta*, to hurry

Ice-shokles—icicles ; cf. Norse, *isjukel*

" And lang *ice-shockles* danglin' doon."
J. S. Bigg.   Alfred Staunton, p. 20

Ike—a diminutive of Isaac

Iky-piky—a corruption of Ipecacuanha

Ill-willy—grudgingly

Intack—an enclosed piece of common   Sw.
intaga, to take in

Jammy-Crane—the Heron *(Ardea cinera)*
Probably so named from its long legs.   Fr. *jambe*

Jam-rags—anything over cooked

Janders—the jaundice

Jannak—honest, straightforward, fair, even.
Sw. *jämka*, to adjust ; *jämn*, even.

Jarble—to splash with mud

Jedder—to tremble, or shake ; cf. *Deddur*

Jemmer—a door hinge.   From Lat. *gemellus.*
(See Way's note to *Gymmow* in Prompt. Parv.)

Jew-trump—the Jew's harp

Jike—to squeak

Jinny-green-Teeth—green converva on pools

Jinny-spinner—an insect *(Tipula)*

Jobey—diminutive of Joseph

Jollop—a semifluid mass of anything ; called
in southern English a *dollop.*

Jope—to splash

Kadge—belly ; lit. a *keg*   Sw. *kagge,* a keg

Keck—to upset

Keckin—spying   Su. G. *kika*   Du. *kijcken*
   "*Kekyyn,* or prively waytyn, INTUOR, OBSERVO."
   Prompt. Parv.

Keckle—to giggle, to laugh ; unsteady

Keish—the stem of an umbelliferous plant,
used by boys for the manufacture of pop-guns.
O. E. *kex.*   W. *cecysen,* hemlock.

Kelk—a blow, to strike.
   "Why, man, she *kelk'd* thee like a log."
   John Stagg.   Cumb. Ball. p. 230.

Ken—to know   A.S. *cunnan*   G. & Du. *kennen*
O. N. *kenna.*
   "Full lile we know his hard griefe of mind,
   And how he did long London to *ken.*"
   The King and a poore Northern Man.
   "Why, don't yaw *ken* me, Mistress Jane ?
   I'm poor Dick, fro' Stanley Green."
   Lanc. Ball. p. 182.

Ken-spak—easy to know ; from O. E. *ken* and
A. S. *specca,* a mark.

Kep—to catch   A.S. *cepan*

"Skurrle, skurrle thee down—I'll *kep* thee—come thy
   ways."
                              Ewan Clark.   Cumb. Ball. p. 155.

Kep-bo—a hand-ball; lit. a catch-ball.

Kerse—a cress   A.S. *cærse*, or *cerse*   Du. *kers*
   "Of paramours ne sette he nat a *kers*."
                              Cant. Tales, l. 3754.

Kersmas—Christmas.   On Christmas eve the
   following lines are sung by boys—
      Git up āld wives an' beàke yer pies,
      It's *Kersmas* day i' t' morning.

Keslop—rennet, a calf's stomach   Sw. *kalflöpe*
   "Ther cheese was teugh as *kezzlup*-skin."
                  Mark Lonsdale.   Cumb. Ball. p. 279.

Kest—a ride; a lift on the way; lit. a cast, as
   "I gat a *kest* in a coup er I wod a' bin teer't."

Ket—carrion, or any kind of filth
   "The flesh of animals that have died of disease.
Su. G. *koett*; Icel. *kvett*, caro."—*Jamieson.*

Ketment—low people   Cf. *ket*

Kettle-o'-fish—to make a mess of anything;
   as "Thou's meeàd a bonny *kettle-o'-fish* on't."

Kill—a kiln   W. *cyl*

Kin—kindred   Icel. *kyn*   A.S. *cyn*
   "This writte was gett fra *kin* to *kin*."
                  Cursor Mundi, Sp. E. Eng. p. 128

Kink—a crease   Du. *kink*, a twist, twirl

Kinkin'—laughing   A.S. *cincung*, laughter

Kipe—to retort   Cf. Eng. *gibe*

Kipper—salmon out of season

"Salmon in the state of spawning.   Teut. *kippen*."
Jamieson.

"*Kippertime*, the space of time between the third and twelfth of May, in which fishing for salmon is forbidden."—*Ash.*

Kirk—church'; frequently met with in the names of places, as *Kirk*-by, Torver *Kirk*-us (church-house).

Kist—a chest or ark   Germ. *kiste*   A.S. *cist*   Su. G. *kista*

"& he with keyes vncloses *kystes* ful mony."
Allit P. B. 1. 1438.

Kittle—to tickle   Du. *kittelen*   Icel. *kitla*   A.S. *citelian*

"Leyll Arthey Todd crap till her back,
An' she brast oot a squeelin';
Be quiet fuil—or dea what tou wull !—
Thou *kittles* me when I's dealin'."
Mark Lonsdale.   Cumb. Ball. p. 276.

Kittlin—a kitten

"In the earlier Wicliffite version, Deut. xxxiii. 22, is thus rendered : 'To Dan he seith, Dan, *keetlyng* of a lyon, (*catulus leonis*, vulg.) shal flow largely fro Basan.'   Palsgrave gives the verb to 'kyttell as a catte dothe, *chatonner*.   Gossype, whan your catte kytelleth, I pray you let me have a *kytlynge (chatton)*'."
Way in Prompt. Parv.

Kith—country   A.S. *cyth*, a region

"Thai ferd al sauf into thair *kyth*."
Cursor Mundi, Sp. E. Eng. p. 132

Kizen't—dried up, parched

"*Kizen*, to shrink, especially in consequence of being exposed to the sun or drought."—*Jamieson.*

Knap—a blow   G. *knappen*, to crack

Kysty—dainty

"Some weshed out their chammer pots—ye may be suer they worn't *kysty*—an' hed 'em filled."
Invasion o' U'ston, p. 6.

Kyte—belly   Icel. *kvithr*   A.S. *cwitha*

"'Their *kytes* weel tugg'd wi' solid gear,
They now began to guzzle."
John Stagg.   Cumb. Ball. p. 200.
"An' theeàr at teàbles heeàd we sat—they fed me like a king,
An' efter blaain' owt mi *kyte*, they ex'd me if I'd sing."
Local Ball. in *Ulverston Mirror*, Sep. 21st, 1867.

Laa—low; law   O.N. *lag*

"With thi *laa* hase made him leyce,
Butte him is lothe to be in pece."
The aww. of K. Arth. st. xxvi. l. 9.

Lad's love—southern-wood

Lafter—one brood of chickens; the number of eggs which a hen sits upon during incubation. Scotch, *lachter*
"Teut. *eyeren legghen*, ova ponere."—*Jamieson.*

La hurr—see the hare; A.S. *la*, lo! and *hara*, a hare; an old hunting phrase in Furness.   Probably because the term is not of Anglo-Norman, or French origin, it does not occur in "Le Venery De Twety," a work on hunting and hunting terms, by the chief huntsman to King Edward the Second.   See *Rd. Ant.* v. 1, p. 149.

Lait—to seek   O.N. *leyta*   Icel. *leita*   Sw. *leta*

"Of alle thir, men sal yhelde acount strayt,
   Sal nathyng than be thar to *layt*."
                              Pricke of Conscience, l. 6001.

Laik—play   A.S. *lác*   Mœso. G. *laiks*
Sw. *lek*

"Nae mair he cracks the leave o' th' green,
   The cleverest far abuin ;
But *lakes* at wait-not-whats within,
   Aw Sunday efter-nuin."
                              Relph.   Cumb. Ball. p. 7.
"May luiky dreams *lake* round my head this night,
And show my true-luive to my longing sight."
                              Ewan Clark.   Cumb. Ball. p. 162.

Lakin'—to play   A.S. *lácan*, to play

"*Laykyn*, or thing that chyldryn pley wythe.   *Ludibile.*"—*Prompt. Parv.*

Lang—long   A.S. *lang*   Fris. *lange*   O.N. *langr*

"Whether he lyf *lang* or short while,
   Bot thyng that es wlatsome and vile."
                              Pricke of Conscience, l. 632.

Langin'—longing, desiring   Germ. *verlangen*

"And by swylke thoghtes for to hafe gret desire and *langgyng* to thise vertus."—*Hamp. Prose Treats.* p. 37.
"Cum, Bet, says Jack, let's hev a smack ;
   I've *lang't* for t' boon a week.—
Here, tak it then, says Bet again ;
   An' slap't 'im reet o' th' cheek."
                              North Lonsdale Magazine, p. 109.

Lang Crown—an apocryphal personage who
is said to have outwitted the devil.

"It caps *Lang Crown*, an' he cap't t' ald Lad."
                              T' Invasion ò' U'ston, p. 4.

Langlin'—tying the fore legs of horses, etc.,
to prevent them straying.

"*Langelyn*, or bynd to-gedder. *Colligo.* In the
noth to *langel* signifies to hopple, or fasten the legs
with a thong. To *langle*, in Norfolk, implies to
saunter slowly, as if it were difficult to advance one
foot before the other."—*Way* in Prompt. Parv.

"To Langel—properly to tie together the two
legs of a horse, or other animal, on one side; as, 'to
langel a horse.' Su. G. *lang-a*, to retard."

Jamieson.

Lant—urine; a game at cards   Eng. *loo*

"It wus nowt oth' warld o God boh arron owd
lant."—*Tim Bobbin.*

Lap—to enfold

"*Lappyn*, or whappyn yn clothys (happyn to-gedyr,
wrap togeder in clothes). *Involvo*."—*Prompt. Parv.*

"Bot it be a wyndyng clothe onely,
That sal be *lapped* obout his body."

Pricke of Conscience, l. 841.

Lang-of—on account of   A.S. *gelang*

Lash-kome—a comb for the hair

Lat—a lath   Germ. and Du. *lat*

Lathe—a barn, or store house; "*Lathe*, a
barn." ASH. "*Lathe*, which does not occur in its
proper place in the Promptorium, is possibly a word
of Danish introduction into the eastern counties,
Lade, *horreum*, DAN. Skinner observes that it was
very commonly used in Lincolnshire. It occurs in
Chaucer:

"Why ne hadst thou put the capel in the *lathe*."

Reves Tale.

"*Granarium*, lathe."—*Roy M.S.* 17 c. xvii. "A
lathe, *apotheca*, *horreum*."—*Way* in Prompt. Parv.

"Whyle t' fiddlers they're at wark i' t' *leathe*,
  An' thrang their fiddles tuning."
                    John Stagg.   Cumb. Ball. p. 199.

Lea—a scythe   Sw. *lie*

Leàce—to castigate

Leàk—to look

Leàt—late

Ledder—leather   Dan. *læder*   It is used as a
  term of commendation in the following local rhyme :
    "That's mi lad o' *ledder !*
    When I kill mi cow thou sal hev t' bledder."

Lee—a lie   A.S. *lyge*

Leemers—hazel nuts when ripe, separate
  easily from the husks, and are then called brown
  leemers   Icel. *lima*, to cut away
  "*Leamer, Leemer*, a nut that separates easily from
the husk, as being fully ripe."—*Jamieson.*

Leet—a light, as "day-*leet*;" to alight, as "I
  fell an' *leet* o' my heeàd."

Leister—a fish spear   Su. G. *liuster*
  "We walked to the river side above the bridge,
where all our tenants were assembled with poles and
spears, or rather '*leisters*,' for catching salmon."
        Her Majesty Queen Victoria's "*Journal of our
        Life in the Highlands*," p. 125.

Letter i' t' cannel—a spark in the wick of a
  candle denotes that a letter is coming to the house.

Lever—rather ; from A.S. *leof*, dear, comparative, *leofra.*
  "What? schal I buy it on my fleisch so deere?
    Yet had I *lever* wedde no wyf to yere !"
                    Cant. Tales, l. 5750.

Ley—lea

> "*Ley*, field after the crop is cut, *clover ley*, etc."
> *F. J. Furnivall* in Gloss. to "Hymns to the
> Virgin & Christ."
> "Bi a forest as y gan walke
> With-out a paleys in a *leye*."
> *Hymns to Virgin & Christ*, p. 95.

Lick—to beat

Lig—lie Icel. *liggja* Su. G. *ligga* A.S. *licgan*

> "That ere he came to *lig* in his bed,
> His dog and he full ill did tire."
> *The King and a poore Northern Man.*

Lig-a-leàm—to do bodily injury

Lile—little Dan. *lille*

> "Afoore we gat to U'ston town,
> I pluckt up heart an' spak reet out;
> She leeak't at me—the sweet *lile* lass—
> But what she answered matters nout."
> *J. S. Bigg.* Shifting Scenes, p. 172.

Lily-white-Lady—a spectral apparition, haunting old manorial residences

Lilt—to step lightly; a song

> "Come, Mary, link thi arm i' mine,
> An' *lilt* away wi' me."
> *Waugh's* Lanc. Songs, p. 15.

Lines—a certificate of marriage

Ling—heath (*Calluna vulgaris*) Dan. *lyng*

Lish—smart, active; another form of *lithe*

> "At last some *lish* young souple lads
> Their naigs frae t' steable brought."
> *John Stagg.* Cumb. Ball. p. 201.

Lisk—the groin

"His *leskes* laye alle lene and latheliche to schewe."
Morte Arthure, l. 3280.

List—a border ; selvidge   Du. *lijst* A.S. *list*

" Then I drough me a-mong this drapers· my donet to
   leorne,
To drawe the *lyste* wel along· the lengore hit semede."
Piers Plow. Text A, Pass. v. l. 124.

Loave—offer   Du. *loven*, to praise up, set a
high price on

Lob-sided—unwieldy, with one side heavier
than the other.   South Eng. *lop-sided*, from E. *lobe*

Lock—a quantity ; as, " What a lile *lock* /"

Looàn—a lane   Fris. *lona*

" Across t' green fields an' down t' lang sunny *looans*,
A gud three mile an' mair."
J. S. Bigg. Shifting Scenes, p. 171.

Loppert—coagulated, as *loppered* milk   Sw.
löpe, rennet.

" *Lopered*, coagulated, clotted.   Ps. cxviii. 70 ;
lxvii. 17.   Dan. *löbe*, runnet, from *löbe* to run, run
together, hence to coagulate.   Sw. *löpa i hop*, to curdle."
COLERIDGE.   " *Loper*, coagulated, clotted, thick.
Prov. Dan. *lubber*, anything coagulated.   O.N. *laupa*,
to run, congeal.   O.H. Germ. *leberen*, to coagulate.
Harl. M.S. 4196 reads *lopyrd*."—*Morris* in Gloss. to
Pricke of Conscience.

" Bot wlatsome glet, and *leper* blode."
Pricke of Conscience, l. 459.

Loukin-tangs—an instrument for eradicating
weeds

Loup—to leap   Sw. *löpa*, to run

    " When I'se wi' Nell my heart keeps such a rout,
    It *loups*, and *loups*, as if it wad *loup* out."
              Ewan Clark.   Cumb. Ball. p. 159.

Lounder—to lounge about in idleness

Lounter-pins—to whittle a piece of wood in idleness, is to make *lounter-pins*.

Low—a flame

    "O.N. *logi*   Dan. *lue*, *love*.   A.S. *læg*, *lig*   O.E. *loge*, *leie.*
        And brint in their sinagog fire ful bright,
        The *lowe* it swath sinful downright."
              Gloss. to Pricke of Conscience.

Lucky-beeàn—the small hammer shaped bone *(os hyoides)* of the sheep, which children 'wear in their clogs, or shoes, under the impression that it will bring them luck.

Lug—the ear ; short projectives upon pots, pans, etc. ; to pull the hair ; Sw. *lugga.*

    "Come luive, quo I, I'll waanly tak thee down,
    Stand off, thou gowk ! she answer'd with a frown,
    Then with a spang lowpt down amang the hay.
    I scratch'd my *lug*; what could I dui or say."
             Ewan Clarke.   Cumb. Ball. p. 155.

    " The dish with *lugges* that I do carry here,
    Shews all my living is in good strong beer."
              The Fool of Muncaster.

Lug-an'-a-bite—a children's game.   An apple is thrown to some distance, the boys then run for it, and whoever obtains it first, bites at it until he is compelled to throw it away again by the other boys pulling his hair—and so on until the apple is all eaten.

Luthobut—only look ; lit. *look thou but*

Maa—to mow, cut down

Maak—a maggot   Sw. *mask*
> "*Make*, mathe, wyrm yn the fleshe."
>> *Prompt. Parv.*

Maapment—nonsense
> "*Māp'ment*—Martha—*māp'ment!*
> Thou knā'sn't what thow says—
> Thow fair torments my heart owt
> Wi' thy lile contrairy ways."
> *Author of "Joe and the Geologist."*   North
> Lonsdale Magazine, p. 18.

Mackly-what—in some fashion

Maddle—to confuse, muddle

Maffle—blunder   O.E. *mamelen*, to babble
> "I'll niver git heàm while Bobby's my neàm,
> But *maffle* an' sing till I dee, dee, dee."
> *Author of "Joe and the Geologist."*   T. and R. p. 25.

Maffle-horn—a blunderer

Maid—a clothes horse

Mak—kind, as "Thou's a queer *mak* of a chap."

Maikin—the common yellow iris (*Iris Pseuda-corus*).

Mam—mother   W. *mam*

Manegy—cross, ill-tempered

Manifaads—a particular kind of tripe, the surface of which is covered with *many folds;* the small intestines.
> "An' he laid the *manifaads* down, poor man,
> An' he laid the *manifaads* down."
>> *Old Local Song.*

62

Manish—manage

" But that's a thing ye kna reet weel 'at I cud niver
    manish,
  An' sooa, ses I, if that ye want, I think I'd better
    vanish."
Ulverston Mirror, Sep. 21st, 1867.

Mappen—perhaps ; it may happen

  " *Mappen* I may, it cums, *m'appen* I may ;
    Asteed of Amen, I say *m'appen* I may."
Author of "Joe and the Geologist." Cumb. Ball. p. 426.

Marra—a companion, an equal. Sc. *marrow*

    "I needn't now say any meear,
      It's settled I'se ga'in to Barra,
      An' if I git back seaf an' sound,
      To this sang I'll send ye a *marra*."
Ulverston Mirror, Sep. 14th, 1867.

May-gezzelin'—a fool ; lit. a May-gosling

May-gezzelin' day—the 1st of May, when it
was customary to make fools of people, as on the
1st of April

Melder—a quantity

  " *Melder*, the quantity of meal ground at once.
Icel. *malldr*, molitura, from *mala*, to grind."
Jamieson.
  " Under a pile o' hay they fand sic a *melder* o' meeal
—girt secks full—an' dudn't they lug it owte i' varra
lile time."—*Invasion o' U'ston*, p. 5.

Mell—a mallet ; to meddle   O.Fr. *meslee*

      "For with us he so *mells*
        That within England dwells,
        I wold he were somewhere else."
Skelton's Satire on Wolsey.

Memaws—antics, mouthing

Mense—grace

"O.E. *menske* from A.S. *mennisc*, human." COLE-
RIDGE. "*Mensk*, dignity of conduct ; honour ; dis-
cretion. Icel. *menska*, humanitas."—*Jamieson.*
The Old Saxon has *menniski*, humanity.

> "Some wantin' *mense*, some wantin' sense,
>   An' some their best behaviour."
> > *John Stagg.* Cumb. Ball. p. 195.
>
> "Now some o' t' *menceful* mak·o' fwok,
>   As suin as things were settled,
> When they'd yence hed a decent snack,
>   To set off heamewards fettled."
> > *John Stagg.* Cumb. Ball. p. 201.

Mere—a lake Cp. Winder-*mere*, Butter-*mere*,
Thirl-*mere*, and *Mere* Tarn Du. *meer*, a lake

Merry-begitan—a bastard

Middin—a manure heap, dunghill A.S. *midding*

> " A fouler *myddyng* saw thou never nane,
> Than a man is with flesche and bane."
> > *Pricke of Conscience*, l. 628.

Midge—a term of endearment ; as " Thow
lile *midge*," applied to a child ; anything very small

Miff-maff—nonsense (See Maffle)

Mirk—dark O.N. *myrkr*, darkness

Miscanter—a mis-adventure Cp. O.E. *aunter*,
an adventure

Mismaims—disturbs; as "That's a gud barn;
anybody may tak it up an' it niver *mismaims* itsel'.'
Cf. Sc. *mismae*

Moider—to embarrass, stupify, confuse

> " An' meat, an' drink, an' ither things,
> Reet *moider'd* were amang."
> *John Stagg.*   Cumb. Ball. p. 194.

Moon-leet-flittin—a removal of goods during the night to cheat the landlord

Mooter—a portion of meal, etc., which a miller claims as his fee for grinding the grain. Fr. *mouture*

Moppet—a pet

Mopsy—a term of endearment

> " A little *mopse, puellula.*"—*Prompt. Parv.*   NOTE.

Morgen—mud, dirt; generally applied to the roads—" T' rwoads er o' in a *morgen,*" i.e. covered with mud.   Dan. *mŏg,* muck

Mot—word; " Thow's nea 'casion to put thy *mot* in."

Moudiwarp—the mole *(Talpa vulgaris)* A.S. *mold,* earth, and *weorpan,* to toss about

Muck-sweat—a high state of perspiration

Muffatees—cuffs for the wrists

> " Mittens, either of leather or of knitted worsted, worn by old men.   Icel. *muffa*   Dan. *moffe.*"
> *Jamieson.*

Muggy—drizzly   Icel. *mugga,* mist

Mull—dust

"Flem. *mul, gemul*, dust.   Du. *mullen*, to crumble.
Pl. Du. *mull*, loose earth, dust ; Cf. peat *mull*, the
dust and fragments of peat."
Morris—Gloss. to Allit. Poems.
Compare also Sw. *mull*, mould, dust.
"Gif I mele a lyttel more that *mul* am & askez."
Allit. P. B. l. 736.

Mumle—to mutter Sw. *mumla* Du. *mommelen*

"Of this matere I mihte· *momele* ful longe."
Piers Plow. Text A. Pass. v. l. 21.

Mun—mouth Icel. *mun* Sw. *mun*

"Much maugre his *mun*, he mote nede suffer."
Allit. P. C. l. 44.

Munge—to eat, munch

"Thei han *I-maunget* ouur muche· that maketh
hem grone ofte."
Piers Plow. Text A. Pass. vii. l. 245.

Nagas—an abusive designation for a greedy,
stingy person   Su. Goth. *noga*, stingy   Cf. Sw.
noga, strict, accurate

Naggin—tormenting, as a "naggin" pain
Dan. *nage*, to gnaw

Nar—near

Nather—neither   A.S. *náthor*

Natterin—jangling   Teut. *knoteren*

Neaa—no   A.S. *na*

Neàf—fist   O.N. *hnefi*   Dan. *næve*

"Give me your *neaf* Monsieur Mustard-seed."
Midsummer Night's Dream, Act iv. Sc. 1.
"Sweet knight I kiss thy *neif*."
Second part of *Henry the IV.* Act ii. Sc. 4.

Neavy-nack—a game played by children with marbles, buttons, etc.   The hands, with the object, whatever it may be, are placed behind the back, and the following rhyme is repeated—"*Neavy neavy nack*, whedder hand will ta tak."   (See Neaf.)

"Brough lass lak'd at *neavy-nack*."
Mark Lonsdale.   Cumb. Ball. p. 281.

Neet-Haak—the   night   jar   (*Caprimulgus Europæus*)

Neb—the nose   A.S. *neb*

"Blod was his faire *neb* his wnden depe an wide."
Pol. Rel. and Love P. p. 214.

Nesh—soft, tender   A.S. *nesc*   Germ. *nass*

"In the later Wycliffite version the word occurs as follows, 2 Chron. xxiv. 27 : 'For thou herdist the wordis of the book, and thi herte is maad *neische.*'"
Way in *Prompt. Parv.*

"For to Destroy a Wrang Nayle, otherwise callyd a Corne.   Take wylde tansey, and grynde yt, and make yt *neshe*, & ley it thereto, and it wyl bryng yt owght."—*Pol. Rel. and Love P.* p. 36.

"And the saul mare tender and *nesshe*
Than es the body with the flesshe."
Pricke of Conscience, l. 3110.

Nessle—to nestle   A.S. *nestlian*, to nestle

Nesp—to nip off the stalks of gooseberries previous to preserving or cooking

Niggert—a piece of iron placed at the side of
a fire grate to contract its width and save coals.

" '*Niggards*, iron cheeks to a grate' grose; evidently
from E. *niggard*, as it is a parsimonious plan."

Jamieson.

No'but—only, none-but

"Who may forgive synnes, *nobut* God alone ?"
2 c. *Mark*, 7 v.   (Wycliffe's.)

Noggin—a small measure, about half a gill
Gael. *nagaire*, a noggin

Noggy-wife-threeàd—a   strong   unbleached
thread

Nooàs—nose

"Nease, neese, nose A.S.   Dan. *naese* Su. G.
naesa."—*Jamieson.*

"At Lancaster assizes, some years ago, Mr. (now
Lord) Brougham was cross-examining a witness, who
in some answer used the word humbug.   'Humbug!'
exclaimed Mr. Brougham, 'pray what do you mean
by humbug?'   After some hesitation, the witness re-
plied, 'Why, iv ah were to tell yaw as yaw'd a noice
nooase, aw sud be humbuggin yaw.' "

Harland in Ball. and Songs of Lanc.

Nout—nothing

O—all; of

"There's bin two days this wick 'ot wey'n had nowt
at *o*'."

Harland's Lanc. Ball. p. 217.

Oddments—odds and ends, scraps

Off-comes—strangers

"Eye! eye! Morkim Bay ye *off-comes* ca' t'."
Alfred Staunton, p. 6.

Offen—frequent, often

Ofter—more frequently

O-maks—all kinds, all makes

Owre—over

> " *Owre* a streme of watur clene,
> Hit servyd as a brygge I wene."
>
> *Hall. Dict.*

Outrake—common, near enclosed land   O.E.
rayke, to wander about

" *Outrake* is a common term among shepherds.
When their sheep have a free passage from enclosed
pastures into open and airy grounds, they call it a good
outrake."—*Gloss. to Percy's Reliques.*

Paamus—palm us, give us alms   (See Aamus)

Paeps—a foolish youth; perhaps from *paepes*,
paps

"quhilk noe man, I trow, can deny that ever suked
the *paepes* of reason."

> *Orth. and Con. of Brit. Tongue.*

Paddock—applied indiscriminately to the
toad and frog   Icel. *padda*   Du. *padde*

The strange diet of the natives of Taracounte, in
India, is thus described :—

> " Evetis, and snakes, and *paddokes* brode,
> That heom thoughte mete gode."
>
> *King Alis.* v. 6126.

In the later Wycliffite version, the frogs that came
upon the land of Egypt, Exodus viii. 6., are called
Paddockis.

"Paddocke, *crapavlt.* My belly crowleth (croulle)
I wene there be some paddockes in it (grenouilles)
PALSG."—*Way* in Prompt. Parv.

" *Paddock* calls."—*Macbeth,* Act I, sc. I, l. 9.

Paddock-steeàl—a fungus, toad-stool

"A padokstole, *boletus, fungus, tuber, trusca*, asperagus.   CATH. ANG.   Gerarde calls *Fungi* paddock stooles.   Teut. *padden-stoele.*"—*Way* in Prompt. Parv.

Palliass—a straw mattress   Fr. *paillasse*, a straw bed

Parlish—terrible, perilous, used as an intensifying term

"O 'tis a *parlous* boy."
Richard III. Act 3, sc. 1, l. 154.

"Thou art in a *parlous* state, shepherd."
As you Like it, Act 3, sc. 2, l. 45.

"Thus Hercules, that ballats say,
Made *parlish* monsters stoop."
Relph.   Cumb. Ball. p. 8.

"That some day suin at Skinburness
They'd hev a *parlish* bout."
John Stagg.   Cumb. Ball. p. 194.

Parrock—an enclosure

"Parrok, or cowle.   SAGINARIUM.   Parrocke, a lytell parke."   PALSG.—*Prompt. Parv.*

"Parrock, a small enclosure.   A.S. *pearroc.*"
Jamieson.

Pash—a fall, a blow, "a girt *pash* o' rain."
Cp. Dan. *baske*, to slap

"I'll *pash* him o'er the face."
Troil. and Cress. Act 2, sc. 3, l. 213.

"Piries and Plomtres· weore *passchet* to the grounde."—*Piers Plow.* Text A, Pass. v. l. 16.

Paupin'—moving about awkwardly

Peeakin—peeping

Peedlin'—creeping about slyly

Peàt—turf; a pet, a term of endearment, as
"Thow lile *peàt.*"

> " A pretty *peat!* it is best
> Put finger in the eye, an she knew why."
> *Tam. of Shrew*, Act I, sc. I, l. 78.

Peewit—the Lapwing

Pee-wittal—to micturate; always applied to
children

Pelt—the skin   Germ. *pelz*

Pelter—to be in a passion   The G. *pelzen*
means to beat, abuse

Pen-fed—stall-fed

> " My polyle that is *penne-fed* & partrykes bothe."
> *Allit. P. B.* l. 5.

Pester—to annoy, torment   O.Fr. *empestrer*

Pey-swads—the husks or shells of peas

Pesz-meeàl cobble—whinstone, geologically
known as greenstone

Pick, or Puke—to vomit, throw up; Shakspeare uses *puking*

Pick-dark—dark as pitch.   Jamieson gives
" *Pick-black*—black as pitch."   A.S. *pic,* pitch
> " While the neet was dark as *pick.*"
> *John Stagg.*   Cumb. Ball. p. 244

Piggin—a small wooden pail   Gael. *pigean*
> " They drank in *piggins,* pints, or quarts,
> Or ought that com' to han'."
> *John Stagg.*   Cumb. Ball. p. 200

Pig-nuts—earth nuts, the root of an umbelli-
ferous plant *(Bunium flexuosum)*
"And I with my long nails will dig thee *pig-nuts.*"
Tempest, Act 2, sc. 2, l. 172.

Pigsy—a term of endearment, as "Thow lile
pigsy."   A.S. *piga*, a little maid   Dan. *pige*

Pike—pick   A.S. *pycan*   Dan. *pikke*
" *Pike* not thi nose, and in especiall
  Be right well ware, and set hereon thi thought,
  To-for thi soverain cracche ne rube nought."
"Stans Puer ad Mensam."   *Rel. Ant.* v. 1, p. 157.

Pilliver—the covering of a pillow, and sometimes the pillow itself; from A.S. *pile*, a pillow,
and Dan. *vaar*, a case
" For in his male he hadde a *pilwebeer.*"
Cant. Tales, 696.

Pinder—to burn, to over-roast meat   A.S.
pinung, a pining, wasting away.

Pippens—the seeds of the apple, pear, etc.
Dan. *piplinger*, pippins.   The black pippins of the
apple are used, by the country youths and maidens,
as a charm to tell in what direction their future wife
or husband lies.   The fresh pippins are used, and
are pressed between the finger and thumb until they
fly, the following verse being repeated meanwhile :—
   " *Pippin pippin* paradise,
     Tell me where my love lies ; .
     East, west, north, south,
     Kirkby, Kendal, Cockermouth?"
Relph of Sebergham, about 130 years ago thus
alludes to the custom, in his inimitable "St. Agnes'
Fast ; or the Amorous Maiden"—
" A *pippin* frae an apple fair I cut,
And clwose atween my thoom and finger put :
Then cry'd, where wons my luive, come tell me true ;
And even forret straight away it flew."
Cumb. Ball. p. 24.

Pissebed—the dandelion

Pissemire—the ant *(Formica)* Fries. *pisimme*
Du. *pis-miere*, so called from its discharging moisture
like urine ; *pis*, urine, and *mier*, an ant
"He is angry as a *pissemyre*."—*Cant. Tales*, l. 7407.

Plain as a pike staff—a phrase of very common
occurrence, said of anything that is self-evident.
" 'Why silent, luive? and why that blushing cheek!
I hope 'tis right plain English that I speak.'
'*Plain as a pike staff*—but what need I say?
I'se ready, and have been this monie a day.'"
Ewan Clark.   Cumb. Ball. p. 162.

Pleany-pyat—a tell tale

Pobbies—porridge   W. *pobi*, to bake
" We'r short o' *pobbies* fer ar Joe,
But that of course tha didn't know,
Did ta lad ? "
Laycock.   Welcome Bonny Brid.

Pooàk—a bag or sack   A.S. *pocca*, a pouch
or bag
" In a *poke* ful and blac
Sone he caste him on his bac."
Havelok, l. 555.

Poppet—a term of endearment, a doll   Fr.
poupee, a puppet, a baby
"Papyn, chylde of clowtys.   *Pupa.*"
Prompt. Parv.

"Forby gives the word poppin, a puppet, and
poppin-shew, as still retained in use in Norfolk.   He
supposes it to be derived from '*Popin*, spruce, neat,
briske, prettie.'   It may more properly, perhaps, be
derived from *poupon*, a baby.   '*Popet* for childre to
play with, *poopée.*' PALSG."—*Way* in Prompt. Parv.

Pordy—short and fat   Sw. *pösa*, to swell

Porse—a purse   O. Fr. *borse*
> "And lyk a letherne *pors*· lullede his chekes."
> *Piers Plowman*, Text A, Pass. v. l. 110.

Porsy—short of breath   O. Fr. *poussif*, broken winded

Pouk—a pock or bleb on the skin, a boil   A.S. *pocca*, a pouch

Pot-skaar—a piece of broken pottery   Dan. *potteskaar*, a potsherd

Pow-cat—the Polecat *(mustela putorius)*; an animal which emits a strong disagreeable smell, hence the phrase, to "stink like a *pow-cat.*"   O. Fr. *pulent*, stinking

Prog—to thrust   W. *procio*

Proker—poker   W. *procio*, to thrust

Puddin-kite—an unfledged bird

Pudgy—fat   W. *pwg*, a swelling

Puke—to vomit   Cf. Germ. *spucken*, to spit

Pum—the implement (a kind of bat) with which the knur is struck in the game of "Spell and Knur."

Pummer—very large

Pund—a pound   Su. G. *pund*

Pun-faad—pinfold, or pound for cattle which have been found straying   A.S. *pyndan*, to hinder, to pound, shut in ; and *fald*, a fold

Put—to butt with the head W. *pwtio*, to push

"To put, or push, as with the head or horns, a verb still in use in Yorkshire, has been derived from Fr. *bouter*, to butt."—*Way* in Prompt. Parv.

Pyannet—a Magpie, sometimes called Pyat
Gael. *pighaidi* W. *pioden*

Quindam—a fifteenth; evidently a corruption of Lat. *Quindecem*, fifteen. My authority for giving this as a word used in Furness, is the Rev. J. Park, of Walney Island, who has favoured me with the following excerpt from the Church Book. "The poor Tax is charged in Dalton by the Lord's Rent—every 3*s*. 4*d*. Lord's Rent pays ½*g*. at the *Quindam*—1783 poor Tax 160 *Quindams*. S. Hunter pays towards the poor Tax 4*s*. 2*d*. equal to Lord's Rent—my proportion being 1.25 Farthg. at the Quindam."

Mr. Park informs me that so late as 1826 the rate was assessed at 400 *Quindams*.

A tax called the Fiftene is thus spoken of in the old poem "God Spede the Plough" written about 1500 A. D.

> "To paye the Fiftene ayenst our ease,
> Besides the lordys rente of our londe."

Raa—uncooked; damp and chill Dan. *raa*

Raake—to hawk and spit A.S. *hrœcan*
Icel. *kraka*

Rabblement—rabble Lat. *rabula*, a brawler

Rackle—hasty, rash Icel. *rakkr*, bold

> "Wost thou whereof a *racle* tonge serveth?
> Right as a swerd for-kutteth and for-kerveth
> An arm atuo, my dere sone, right so
> A tonge cutteth frendschip al atuo."
>
> *Cant. Tales*, ll. 17271-4.

Raffle—to entangle Du. *rafelen*

Rag—hoar frost; perhaps from A.S. *ragu*, blight, mildew

Rakein—gadding about   Su. G. *reka*, to roam   Icel. *reika*

Ram—rank, high flavoured   Dan. *ram*, rank, rancid

Ramps—wild onions *(Allium ursinum)*

"Linnæus informs us, that the allium ursinum is Gotlandis *rams*, Scanis *ramsk*, W. Gothis *ramsloek*. The word is immediately allied to A.S. *hramsa*, *hramse*, allium sylvestre, vel allium ursinum.   But the common origin is most probably Su. G. *ram*, Icel. *ramr*, olidus, strong, harsh, rank, from its strong smell."—*Jamieson.*

Ramison—a long tedious tale; small talk   Dan. *en lang ramse*, a long rabblement.   "He'd a girt lang *ramison* to tell."

Randy-ruet—a blast upon a horn; to break wind

"And Bleuh the *Ronde Ruwet·* atte Rugge-bones ende."
Piers Plowman, Text A, Pass. v. l. 193.

Rannel-bauk—a cross beam in the chimney

Ratch—to stretch   A.S. *ræcan*, to reach

Ratten—a rat   Gael. *radan*   Span. *raton*

"Ratun or raton.   *Rato, sorex.*"—*Prompt. Parv.*
"I comawnde alle the *ratons* that are here abowte,
That non dwelle in this place with-inne ne with-owte."
Pol. Relig. and Love P. p. 23, l. 1.

Ratton-creak—a hook suspended from the rannel-bauk, on which cooking utensils are hung

Rawky—damp, foggy   Icel. *rakr*
  "Roky, or mysty.   *nebulosus.*"—*Prompt. Parv.*

Reàsty—rancid; usually applied to bacon
  "Reest as flesche (resty) *Rancidus.*"
Prompt. Parv.
  " And for to seche so ferre a lytill bakon **flyk**,
    Which hath long hanggid *resty* and tow."
Rel. Ant. v. 2, p. 29.

Rear—under-done meat, half cooked   A.S.
hrêre, raw

Reir—to laugh   Fr. *rire*   Lat. *ridere*

Recklin—the last of a litter, which is generally
  the smallest.   The term is frequently applied to a
  puny child; from Dan. *vrage*, to cast out, reject

Red-raddle—soft fibrous iron ore *(hæmatite)*,
  used by builders, etc. for marking wood   W. *rhuddel*,
  a ruddy hue

Reeden—cross-tempered
  " If ya cud co what that lile *reedan* paddock meead
podish."—*Sp. West. Dial.* p. 14.

Reet—right; a wright, as mill-*reet*, wheel-*reet*

Render—to melt down suet or fat of any kind
  Icel. *renna*, to cause to run

Rew—to repent   A.S. *hreowan*

Riddle-breeàd—sour cakes made from thin
  dough or batter which has been allowed to stand
  until acetous fermentation has set in   O.E. *cribil*, a
  riddle or seive
  "Panis cribarius, *cribil brede.*"—*Rel. Ant.* v. 1, p. 9.

Riff-raff—sweepings, a reduplicate form of *raff*, refuse, rubbish Germ. *raffen*, to sweep (See Rip-rap)

Rift—to belch Dan. *ræbe*

Rin—run Moes. G. *rinnan*

Rip-rap—a worthless person Dan. *rip-raps*, the rascality

Rive-rags—a destructive child Sw. *rifva*, to pull asunder

Roàn-tree—mountain ash *(Pyrus aucuparia)* Sw. *rönn*, mountain ash

Robin-run i' th' hedge—goose grass *(Galium aparine)*

Rone—the roe of fish Suio. G. *ron* Dan. *rogn*, spawn

Rooky—smoky A.S. *reac, réc*, smoke

Rooar—to roar, cry loudly A.S. *rarian*

Roum—room A.S. *rúm*
"Mony renischche renkez, & yet is *roum* more."
Allit. P. B. l. 96.

Rowly-powly—a rolled dumpling, made of flour and suet

Ruck—a heap A.S. *ricg* O.N. *hruka*, a pile Su. G. *roek*

Rumshun—a disturbance Icel. *rumr*, a noise Cf. O.E. *rem*, an outcry

Ruttlin'—a rattling in the throat   Du. *reutelen*
"And thin hond quaket : and thin throte *ruteleigh*."
Pol. Relig. and Love P. p. 221.
"& his teth shulle Ratelen.
& his throte shal *Rotelen*."
Ibid. p. 224.

Saa—saw; to saw; to sow   Icel. *sa*   Dan. *saae*

Sackless—useless   A.S. *sacleas*, innocent
Icel. *saklauss*, useless   Sc. *sackless*
"Schal synful & *sakles* suffer al on payne."
Allit. P. B. L 716.

Sad—firm   W. *sadiaw*, to make firm.   When
the flesh of a child is firm it is said to be "as *sad's*
a boorde."   Unfermented bread is also called "*sad*
bread."

Sal—shall
"For I *sal* se thine hevenes hegh,
And werkes of thine fingres slegh."
Met. Eng. Psalter, viii. v. 4, Sp. E. Eng. p. 82.

Saim—lard   W. *saim*, grease   Fr. *saindoux*,
hog's lard   O. Fr. *sain*, lard   Span. *sain*, lard,
whence vb. *sainar*, to fatten, and sb. *sainete*, a taste
of grease, a relish.   Cf. Germ. *seim*, any viscous
fluid, such as honey ; also used of *slime*.
"Ge ne schulen eoten flesch ne *saim* bute i muche
secneise."—*The Ancren Riwle*, Rel. Ant. v. 2, p. 1.
When Jonah was swallowed by the whale, according
to one of our old Lancashire poets of the 14th century,
he—
"Stod vp in his stomak, that stank as the deuel ;
Ther in *saym* & in sorghe that sauoured as helle."
Allit. P. C. ll. 274-5.

Sampleth—a piece of needlework ; corrupted
from Sampler   Lat. *exemplar*

Sang—a song   A.S. *sang*

> " For thai sal here thar aungel *sang*,
>   And the haly men sal ay syng omang."
>> *Pricke of Conscience*, ll. 9254-5.

Santer—to walk slowly, saunter

Sap-heeàd—a soft person   A.S. *sæp*, sap

Sap-whissel—a whistle made by boys, of willow, when the sap is running.   After the small branches are cut to the proper form the bark is notched round with a knife, it is then beat on the knee with the knife haft, and the following lines are repeated :—

> " Sip sap, sip sap,
>   Willie, Willie Whitecap."

Sarra—serve

> " And uncle Megs has sent us beef
>   Will *sarra* us aw at dinner."
>> *Miss Blamire.*   Cumb. Ball. p. 55.

Scablins—broken stones   Icel. *skapa*, to shape Cf. Dan. *skabe*

Schooder—the shoulder   Du. *schouder*   Dan. *skulder*   Sw. *skuldra*

Scop—a blow   Du. *schop*, a kick

Scop'rel—a circular disc of bone, which when covered with cloth formed a button   A.S. *scapan*, to form.   A spinner, or tee-totum, was frequently made from these discs—hence the origin of the phrase "I'll meàk the' spin like a *scop'rel.*"

> "Thae turns me mazy.   Thae'rt war nor a *scopperil.*"
>> *Waugh.*   Tufts of Heather, p. 211.

Scorrik—a fragment of anything

Scoup—a ladle

"I laade water with a *scoup* or any other thyng out of a dytche or pytte."—*Prompt. Parv.* p. 283.

Scouder—hurry, confusion

Scraffle—an affray; to struggle   O.N. *skreflas*, to keep one's feet with difficulty

> " Keep up thy heart—ne'er fear !
> Our bits o' bairns 'll *scraffle* up,
> Sae dry that sworry tear."
> > *Anderson.*   Cumb. Ball. p. 306.

Scram—the rind of cheese

Scrat—scratch   Du. *kratsen*

> " And ilk ane *scratte* other in the face,
> And thair awen flessch of-ryve and race."
> > *Pricke of Conscience,* l. 7378.

Scratchins—the refuse of lard or tallow after melting

Screed—a shred, a rag   A.S. *screade*, a shred Icel. *skridna*, to be torn

Scree—a shingly place on a hill side

Scroggs—a rocky place abounding with stunted trees, as "Urswick *Scroggs*," near Ulverston   Germ. *schräg*, crooked   A.S. *scrob*, a shrub   Dan. *skrog*, a shrivelled carcase

"Discoveres now sekerly *skrogges* and other,
That no skathelle in the *skroggez* skorne us here-aftyre."
> *Morte Arthure,* ll. 1641-2.

Scroo—to slide

Scrud—any portion of clothing, as "He hedn't a *scrud* on him."   A.S. *scrūd*, clothing

Scrow—in an untidy state

Scuff—nape of the neck

Scufter—in a hurry   Cf. Eng. *scuffle*

Scun—to throw, to fly through the air, to run
swiftly   Cf. Eng. *scud* and *skim*

Seàf—certain, safe   W. *sef*

Seàn—soon

Seàp—soap   Lat. *sapo*

Seàr—a sore; painful   Su. G. *saar*   Icel. and
A.S. *sar*, a sore, wound

Seater—any garment worn so thin as to be
almost in holes, is said to be "o' in a *seater*."   O.N.
sigti, Dan. *sigte*, Sw. *sikt*, a sieve

Seaves—rushes   Sw. *säf*   Dan. *siv*, a rush

Seàv—to save

Seav-o'—save all; a box with a narrow opening
through which children drop their money (savings)

Sebben—seven   Germ. *sieben*

Sed—said
   "I'se neither am blinde nor drunke, he *sed*."
            The King and a Poor Northerne Man.

Seeà-Pye—the Oyster-Catcher

Seeà-Maa—Sea-Mew, any of the Gulls

Sek—sack   Du. *sak, sek*   Dan. *sæk*   W. *sac*
"*Sek*, of clothe or lethyr.   *sacus*."—*Prompt. Parv.*
"On a *sek* ful of fedyrs, for scho schuld syt soft."
Tourn. of Tott.   Percy's Rel. p. 93, l. 76.

Selt—sold

Semple—poor, as in the phrase "gentle and semple"—rich and poor

Sen'—since
"It's nobbut this time last year, come tomorn,
Sen' me an' Polly walkt to U'ston fair."
Stanyan Bigg.   Shifting Scenes, p. 171.

Service-silver—an old manorial tax, payable when the heir to the manor attains his majority.   It is now said to be for the purchase of silver spoons.

Settle—a seat, or bench   A.S. *setl*, seat, bench, or stool

Shaff—pshaw, nonsense

Shafflin—vacillating, prevaricating   E. *shuffle*

Sham—shame
"For when they pray,
Ye shall have nay,
What so they sey,
be ware, ffor *sham!*"
Rel. Ant. v. 1, p. 23.

Shandry-dan—a cart fitted up with springs

Shap—shape
"Therfor bide at home, what so ever hap,
Tylle the world be turnyd into another *shap*."
Rel. Ant. v. 2, p. 29.

Shede—to part the hair

"To *shede* one's heed, parte the heares evyn from the crown to the myddes of the foreheed. PALSG. From the Ang. Sax. *sceadan*, separarere."
Way in Prompt. Parv. p. 188.

Sheule—to walk with a shuffling gait

"To schayle, *degradi, et degredi.* CATH. ANG. Schayler, that gothe croked with his legges, *ge vas eschays.* I *shayle* with the fete, gentretaille des pieds. PALSG."—*Way* in Prompt. Parv.

Shilla—the small pebbles on the beach

Shive—a slice of bread   Germ. *scheibe*   Dan. *skive*, a slice

"And of your softe breede but a *schivere.*"
Cant. Tales, l. 7422.

Shool—a spade

Shuppen—a cow house   A.S. *scypen*, a stall, stable

"Lang afoore we saaw t'leet,
He was fashing hard ;
Indure, out o' dure,
I' *shuppen*, field, an' yard."
Stanyan Bigg.   Shifting Scenes, p. 170.

Sic—such

"For t' time flang by at *sic* a reate,
Titter nor wings o' birds."
Stanyan Bigg.   Shifting Scenes, p. 171.

Sic-an-sic-like—all of a character

Sile—to strain, or filter   Sw. *sila*

Sind—to rinse or wash

"*Synd*, to *synd* down one's meat."—*Jamieson.*
"O.N. *sund*, swimming."—*Atkinson.*

Sipe—to drain ; also to drink, as "*Sipe* it off"
W. *sipiaw*, to sip   Platt. D. *sipen*, to ooze, trickle

Skaar—fear   Icel. *skjarr*, fearful, timid
Su. G. *sky*, terror, horror

Skell—shell

Skelp—a blow   Icel. *skelfa*, to strike   Gael.
sgeilp, a stroke   "A *skelp* on t' lug."

Skelter—to run quickly   Sw. *skala*, to scamper

Sken—to squint ; to look slyly with the eyes
  " 'Let's see, isn't that him 'at *skens* a bit ?'   'A bit,
says ta, lass?   It's aboon a bit, by Guy.   He *skens* ill
enough to crack a looking glass, welly.   His e'e-seet
crosses somewhear abeawt th' end on his nose.' "
            Waugh.   Sketches of Lanc. Life, p. 25.
  " Aw'll may sombry *sken* abeawt that jackass o'
mine."—*Waugh.*   Tufts of Heather, p. 94.

Skiander—to disperse, spread about   A.S. *scylan*

Skift—to remove   Sw. *skifta*   Dan. *skifte*
  "Loke ye *skyfte* it so that us no skathe lympe."
                  Morte Arthure, l. 1643.
    " & oft bothe blysse & blunder
      Ful skete hatz *skyfted* synne."
  Sir Gaw. and Green Knt.   Sp. E. Eng. p. 220.

Skilf—a shelf   A.S. *scylfe*, a shelf   Cf. Sc. *skelf*

Skirl—to cry, to call loudly   Su. G. *skörl*, an
  outcry

Skitters—diarrhœa   Icel. *skitr*

Skoggars—a covering for the arms, to protect them from being sun-burned. They were usually made of old stockings with the feet cut off Su. G. *skugga*, a shade Icel. *skygga*, to shade Cf. Sc. *skug*, a shade, what defends from heat

Slaa—slow A.S. *sláw*

Sleea—the fruit of the black thorn A.S. *slá* Dan. *slaa*

Sleea-worm—the slow worm or blind worm (*Anguis fragilis*)

Slaak—to work in a dirty or slovenly manner; to slobber and kiss Su. G. *slaska*, to make sloppy

Sláir—to move about in an indolent way

Slamp—soft, loose Dan. *slap*, loose "This barne mun be badly, it fleish's varra *slamp*."
"But what's up witho? Thae looks very *slamp* abeawt th' face."—*Waugh.* Tufts of Heather, p. 32.

Slape—smooth, slippery, bare A "*slape* feàce" is one devoid of whiskers. "*Slape* scope," a bald head. "T' ice is varra *slape*"—smooth and slippery O.N. *sleipr*

Slapper—any large object

Slash—wet; miry, as "a varra *slashy* day." Dan. *slaske* Sw. *slask* Su. G. *slaska*

Slatter—to spill water about

Sledder—to move slowly

Sleeveless—useless
"He thinks o' nought i' th' world but race-runnin', an' wrostlin', an' pigeon flyin', an' sich like *sleeveless* wark."—*Waugh.* Tufts of Heather, p. 319.

Slipe—a stroke; to drink, as "*Slipe* off thi glass an' cu' thi ways;" also to cheat
"Slouen alle at a *slype* that served ther-inne."
Allit. P. B. l. 1264

Slobber—to make a noise in eating

Slocken—to quench thirst; to cool hot iron, or the fire   Cf. Su. G. *slockna*   Sw. *slockna*, to be extinguished
"*Sloknynge*, or quenchyng."—*Prompt. Parv.*

Slonk—a lazy slinking fellow

Slotch—a drunken character   Cf. O.N. *slaki, slókr*, an inactive, dull person

Sluff—the skin of a gooseberry

Slutch—mud   W. *yslwch*   A.S. *slog*, slough
When Jonah was cast forth from the whale's belly we are told :—
"Thenne he swepe to the sonde in *sluchched* clothes."
Allit. P. C. l. 341.

Smack—a blow with the open palm, as "I'll *smack* thi mouth."

Smiddy—a smith's shop   Sw. *smedja*, a smithy   Su. G. *smida*, to smite

Smittal—infectious, contagious   W. *ysmotiau*, to spot   Dan. *smitsom*, infectious   Belg. *smettelick*

Smooar—to smother   A.S. *smorian*
"He *smorit* thame with smuke."
Gloss. to *Pricke of Conscience.*

Snail's-trot—a slow pace

Snaa—snow   A.S. *snáw*

Snape—to snub, check   Icel. *sneipa*   Dan.
snibbe, to answer anyone sharply   Cf. snip, nip, &c.
" Ur laverd *snaips* thir tua tuns."
                    Notes to *Pricke of Conscience*, p. 268.

Snarled—entangled, twisted   Dan. *snære*, a
snare ; *snöre*, a lace
" Palsgrave gives the verb ' I snarle, I strangle in a
halter, or corde, *Jé estrangle:* My greyhounde had
almost *snarled* hym selfe to night in his own leesse.'
See Forby's Norfolk Dialect, v. 'Snarl, to twist, entangle, and knot together as a skein.'"
                        Way in Prompt. Parv.
" And from her head oft rent her *snarled* hair."
                Spencer's Fairy Queen, B. iii. Canto xii.

Sneck—the latch of a door or gate
"Their kisses just sound like the *sneck* of a yett."
                    Anderson.   Cumb. Ball. p. 339.

Snerl—to turn up the nose in contempt, as
"Thow needn't *snerl* up thi nooàs, I'se as gud as
thee."   Dan. *snerpe*, to wrinkle   Sw. *knorla*, to
twist, to curl

Snerp—to shrivel up · Dan. *snerpes*, to grow
contracted   Sw. *snörpa*
"I *snurpe*, I snobbe, I sneipe on snoute."
Poem on Old Age 14th Cent.   Rel. Ant. v. 2, p. 211.

Snert—to emit a sound from the nose in
mockery or scorn, as "*Snertin*' an' laffin'."
"*Snvrtyn*, or frowne wythe the nese for scorne or
shrewdenesse. *Nario.*"—*Prompt Parv.* Cf. *snort*

Snifters—a cold in the head, accompanied by
snuffling in the nose   Su. G. *snyfsta, snyfta*, to sniff.

Snifter—a cold wind; a cold day

> "Icel. *snæfur*, frigidus, austerus."—*Jamieson*.
> "He got a gey *snifter* gain' our the muir."
> *Gregor*.   Dialect of Banffshire.

Snod—neat, trim   O.N. *snodinn*   N. *snöydd*, made smooth

Snot—mucus from the nose   A.S. *snote*   Dan. *snot*

> "His neys smellid of the Jew's *snot* and foul spitting."
> Gloss. to *Pricke of Conscience*, p. 318.

Snotty—a dirty person; a saucy fellow

Snout-band—a piece of sheet iron nailed upon the front (snout) of a clog sole.   In South Lancashire the neat clogs of the factory girls are snouted with brass

Sogram—a person inactive through fatness W. *soegen*, a swaggy female; *soeglyd*, puffed   Gael. *seachran*   Ex. "Thow lile fat *sogram*."   "That barne's a fair *sogram*."

Sooa-sooa—be quiet, as "*Sooa, sooa*, barnes"

Soople—pliant, flexible; a thrashing, as "I'll *soople* thi hide for thè."   Sc. *souple*   Fr. *souple* Gael. *subailt*

Soppy—wet, plastic, sloppy

Soss—the sound caused by a soft body falling; "I cud hear t' *soss*."   "I tummelt wi' sic a *soss* on t' ice."

Sotter—to boil slowly; the sound emitted in boiling by any thick substance, as oatmeal porridge A.S. *seothan*, to seethe

Sōtus—Salt-house, the name of a hamlet near Ulverston

Souk—to suck   A.S. *sucan*

> " Thai sal for threst the hevedes *souke*
>   Of the nedders that on tham sal rouke."
> > *Pricke of Conscience*, l. 6764.

> " The cradil at hire beddes feet is set,
>   To rokken, and to give the child to *souke*."
> > *Cant. Tales*, l. 4154.

> " Surge mea sponsa, swete in sight,
>   And see thi sone thou gafe *souke* so scheene."
> > *Hymns to the Virgin and Christ*, p. 1.

So'der—to join, to solder   W. *sawdrio*

Sour-dock—wild Sorrel

> " *Sowre Dokke* (herbe)."—*Prompt. Parv.*

Sowen—very great

Span-new—quite new

> " *Spannew*, lit. 'as new as a chip,' from A.S. *spón*, a chip; cf. Swed. *spillerney*—span new, with Sw. *spiltra*, a splinter, and Eng. spill."—*Coleridge.*

Spang-wiew—"To place anything on one end of a board, the middle of which rests on a wall, and strike the other end smartly, so as to make it start suddenly up, and fling what is upon it violently aloft."—*Jamieson.*   Seldom done to anything but Toads or Frogs

Sparrabls—Sparrow-bills, small nails used by shoemakers

Speåd—a spade   A.S. *spåd*

Speal-beeån—the small bone of the leg *(Fibula)*   A.S. *spelc*, a splint

Spean'd—wean'd, as "Mally, hev ye *spean'd* that barne yet." Halliwell gives *Speans*, as used in Kent for teats A.S. *spana*, teats Sw. *spene*, a teat

Spell—a portion of time, as "He's hed a lang *spell* on't." A.S. *spelung*, a turn, change

Spink—the *Emberiza Citrinella* W. *pinc*

Spittin'—a slight shower

Sprag—to chock a wheel by putting a piece of wood in the spokes

Sprint—a short race; a spring at the end of a race

Sprod—the young of salmon

Sproguin—strutting; wandering, or rambling about
Cf. "'*Sproaging*, courtship under the shade of night;' and '*To Sprog, Sproag*, to make love under the covert of night.' A.S. *spreocan*, loqui Su. G. *sprok*, colloquium."—*Jamieson*.

Sprush—to deck; to put in order; to dress up in best clothes Cf. Eng. *spruce* Sc. *sprush*
"Geh 'wa an' *sprush* yirsel up."
Gregor. Dialect of Banffshire.

Spy-eye—I spy; a children's game

Squib—half a glass of any liquor, as "a *squib* o' gin."
"Seeah efter he'd keearfully lapt up his dibs,
As a sooart o' resate he steead for *squibs*."
Sp. West. Dial. p. 24

Squeel—to scream

Stang—a cart shaft   Icel. *staung*   Dan. *stang*
Belg. *stange*

Stang—the sting of a Bee or Wasp   " Icel.
stanga, pungere."

Stang—a pole.   To ride the stang was a
punishment "intended for those husbands who beat
their wives."   If the culprit could not be laid hold
of, a boy was placed on the pole or ladder, and carried shoulder high round the town or village, and on
the route he chaunted a doggrel rhyme such as the
following :—
    " It isn't for my part 'at I ride this *stang* ;
      It is for Johnny Johnson 'at hes done wrang."
Should the victim be a woman, who having assumed
the breeches, asserts her right to wear them by
knocking her liege lord down, the rhyme would be
something like the following :—
    " Ting tang to the sign of the pan !
      Our good neighbour's wife
      She has beat her goodman."
Jamieson says "a henpecked husband was also sub-
jected to this punishment."   Su. G. *nidstaeng*, the
pole of infamy

Stank—a ditch or pool   Su. G. *staang*

Steán—a stone ; a 14lb. weight   A.S. *stan*
Su. G. *sten*   Icel. *steinn*

Steán-chek—the wheat-ear   Sw. *stensqvätta*

Stee—a stile; a ladder   Dan. *stige*   Icel. *stigr*
A.S. *stigan*, to ascend ; *stæger*, a stair

Stegg—a gander   Icel. *steggr*   N. *stegg*, a male
bird
      " An' its a *steg*
      That's lost its leg."
          Nursery Rhyme.

Steeák—to shut, to fasten ; to secure with a
stake   A. S. *stician*, to stick in   Germ. *stecken*
"& when ye arn staued, styfly *stekez* yow therinne."
Allit. P. B. l. 352.
"& *steken* the yates ston-harde wyth stalworth barrez."
Ibid. l. 884.
"He *steeks* the fa'-yett softly too."
Anderson.   Cumb. Ball. p. 309.

Stele—a stile or ladder, the diminutive of
stee   (See Stee.)

Stickin'-bit—the neck-end of mutton

Stiddy or Stithie—an anvil   Icel. *stethi*
"Of these, thre be, as it were, hammers stryking,
and the rest *stiddies*, kepping the strakes of the ham-
meres."—*Orth. and Con. of the Brit. Tongue*, p. 12.
"Als it war dintes on a *stethi*,
That smythes smittes in a smethey."
Pricke of Conscience, preface, p. ix.

Stime—to see the faintest form of anything,
as "I can't see a *stime*."   Su. G. *stomme*, an outline
"It was pick dark, ya cuddn't see a stime."
Sp. West. Dial. p. 14.

Stirrup-oil—a flogging with a strap

Stived-up—crowded in a small space   Sw.
stufva, to stew

St. John's Nut—a double hazel nut

Sto'-fed—full to repletion   Germ. *stauen*, to
stow away

Stoo—a stool

Stoop—a post, as "Gate *stoop*"   Su. G. *stolpe*,
a support

Stordy—stiff in opinion, as "Don't be sooä *stordy*, for thow kna's thow's wrang;" a stiff built person, as "He's a rare *stordy* lad" A.S. *stor*, great, vast Dan. *storhed*, bigness

Stotter—to stagger about

Stouk—a sheaf of corn Cf. Germ. *stauche*, a truss or bundle of flax, etc.

Strang—strong, powerful A.S. *strang*
"Be he nevyr so *strang* a thefe."
Rel. Ant. v. 2, p. 109.

Stranger—a flake of carbon fluttering on the fire grate is said to betoken the coming of stranger
"See yo, Sam, a *stranger* uppo th' bar, theer."
Waugh. Sketches of Lanc. Life, p. 28.

Streäk—struck, as "He *streäk* me ower t' lug." Germ. *streichen*

Streäkt—stretched; generally used with *full* or *lang* prefixed, as "*lang* streakt," lying at full length A.S. *streccan*, to make prostrate

Strinkle—to sprinkle; scatter about
"*Strenkelyn*, or sprenkelyn."—*Prompt. Parv.* Cf. *straggle*
"I schal *strenkle* my distresse & strye al togeder."
Allit. P. B. 307.

Stupe—a foolish fellow Lat. *stupeo*, to be stupified

Stutter—to stammer; confusion, as "He wos o' in a *stutter*." Du. *stotteren* Germ. *stottern*

Sudn't—should not

Suff—a drain

Sump—a deep pit, at the shaft foot of a mine
  Dan. *sump*, mire, puddle

Sumph—a soft fellow

Swad—the shell or pod of Peas and Beans
  Du. *swaad* Germ. *schwaden* Cf. Eng. *swathe* and
  swaddle
  "Like peighs i' one *swad*."
                      Waugh. Tufts of Heather, p. 24

Swallow-hooál—holes frequently met with in
  the Limestone of Furness, which *swallow* up all the
  water poured into them.   In some instances the
  water lodges in cavernous fissures of the rock; and
  in others it traverses some distance under ground,
  and then makes its appearance again on the surface.
  It is said that chaff thrown into a Swallow-hole at
  Lindal Moor, re-appears at Yarl-Wells, Dalton, a
  distance of about two miles

Swammel—to climb a pole or tree

Swankin—anything very large

Swanky—small beer, or weak ale; Cf. Wankle
  infra

Swap—to exchange   "Dick thinks he's a gud
  wife, but I wodn't *swap* him for two like his."   Icel.
  skipta, to change

Sward—the rind or skin of bacon
  "*Swarde*, or sworde of flesche (swad or swarde)
  Coriana. A.S. *sweard*, cutis porcina."—*Prompt. Parv.*

Swarm—same as Swammel
  "He *swarmed* up into a tree."—*Syr Isenbras*, 351,
  (Halliwell) Cf. Eng. *worm*, to wriggle, twist

Swash—watery food; another form of *wash*, intensified with the addition of *s*

> " If ye itt 'em when they're *swash*,
> They'll fill yer belly full o' trash."
>> *Lons. Mag.* v. I, p. 512.

Sweal—to flare in burning, as when a candle burns down on one side   A.S. *swélan*, to burn

Swelter'd—over-power'd with heat; melted with heat, as "Bless o', barne, it's parlish yat.   I'se fairly *swelter'd.*"   "It's a *swelterin'* yat day."   A.S. *swélan*, to burn

Swerd—a sword   A.S. *swerd*

Swill—a flat basket   A.S. *swethil*, a swathing band

Swill—to wash down   A.S. *swilian*, to swill, wash

" Here, sup; an' *swill* those hay-seeds eawt o' thi throttle."—*Waugh*.   Tufts of Heather, p. 207.

" Pottes and dyshes for to *swele*,"
>> Sp. E. Eng. p. 117.   *Morris.*

" Ful wel kan ich dishes *swilen.*"
>> *Havelok the Dane*, l. 919.

Swiller—a basket maker

Swin'd—twisted, warped   Dan. *svinde*, to shrink, cockle

Swinger—very big

Ta—thou; to; as "Will *ta* (thou) ga *ta* U'ston fair ?"

Tack—flavour, as "It's a queer *tack* wi' it." Sw. *tag*, a touch

Tackle—to put right; to lay hold of W. *taclu,*
to deck

Taffled—entangled ; another form of *Caffled*

Taggelt—a ragged person ; useless ; always
used as a term of contempt, as "Thow nasty dirty
taggelt." "Thow drukken *taggelt.*" Sw. *taaga,*
a fibre, a tear

Taistrel—a booby; used in the same way as
Taggelt Dan. *tosse*
"Thow drukken *taistrel,* thow."
T' Lebby Beck Dobby, p. 8.
"Up brouc'd the *taistrels* in a leyne."
John Stagg. Cumb. Ball. p. 218.

Tait—a small fluff on the clothes or elsewhere
Icel. *tæta*

Tak—take Icel. *taka*

Tang—a strong flavour
"*Tongge,* or scharpnesse of lycure yn tastyng.
Acumen."—*Prompt. Parv.*
"Forby gives '*Tang,* a strong flavour generally, but
not always an unpleasant one.' Fuller says of the best
oil, 'it hath no tast, that is *tang,* but the natural gust
of oyl.' Skinner derives the word from the Dutch
Tangwe, *acer.*"—*Way* in Ibid.

Tang—a tongue, or that portion of a knife,
fork or other instrument, which is inserted in the
haft A.S. and Dan. *tunge*

Tangle—sea weed Dan. *tang,* sea weed
Du. *tang*

Tangs—a pair of tongs A.S. *tange* Du. *tang*

Tantrum—a rage W. *tant,* a whim or flight

Targus—worthless   Gael. *tair*, contempt

Tarn—a mountain lake   Icel. *tjörn*

Tarrant—an ill-natured, crabbed person   A.S.
torn, anger

Ta-t'-foore—ready prepared; already saved

"An' sum may be *ta t' foore* for t' barns,
When we ga under t' grund."
North Lons. Mag. p. 19.

Ta-yeere—this year; metaphorically, a long
time, or never

"Yit had I lever wedde no wyf *to yere*."
Cant. Tales, l. 5750.

Teeá—toe   A.S. *ta*   Dan. *taa*

Tead-in-a-pot—formerly a common mode of
bewitching any one was to put a toad in a jar, and
cover it closely; as the toad dwindled away, so would
the person bewitched

Tead-spit—same as Cuckoo-spit

Tean—the one, as "Teck t' *tean* an' leav t'
udder;" taken, as "Thow's *tean* my hat asteed o'
thi aan."

Teav—to tumble anything about, to unravel
Dan. *tievsle*, to unravel, unweave

Teddisum—tedious

Teem—to empty, to pour out   Dan. *tom*,
empty, *tömmer*, to make void   Icel. *tómr*, empty

" *Temyn*, or maken empty. *Vacuo, evacuo.*"
Prompt. Parv.

"Tittez tirantez doune, and *temes* theire sadilles."
Morte Arthure, l. 1801.

Teemin'—pouring, as "It's fair rainin' and *teemin'* down."

Telt—told

Terble—terrible

Tew—to tire, fatigue   A.S. *teón*, to tug
Cf. *Toar*

Tewat—the Lapwing   *(Vanellus cristatus.)*

Thack—thatch, a roofing of straw   A.S. *thac*
Icel. *thak*
"He coude *theche* a hous, and daüb a wall."
                    Rel. Ant. v. I, p. 43.

Thible—a porridge stick
   " Her tung—it makes mo fair go cowd,
      Sin th' day hoo broke my nose i' th' fowd
      Wi' th' edge o'th porritch *thible.*"
                    Waugh. Lanc. Songs, p. 44.

Thick-Dicks—a cant expression for thick
porridge

Thimmel-pie—a blow on the head with the
thimble on a woman's finger

Thoum—thumb   Dan. *tomme*
   " Yur *thowmes* berith moch awai."
                    Rel. Ant. v. 2, p. 176.
   " To the *thowme* goth that on branche,
      The cardiacle he wol stanche."
                    Ibid. v. I, p. 190.

Thoum-butter-ceak—an oatmeal cake upon
which the butter is spread with the thumb

Thow's-like—used as an equivalent for "it's only reasonable," as "Eigh, thow mun ga, *thow's like;*" "I knā thow can du it, *thow's like.*"

Thow wastes thy wind—said of any one whose language is unavailing

"*Thou wastist thi wynde* & spillist thi speche,
Thi wordis me is looth to heere."
Hymns to the Virgin and Christ, p. 67.

Thra—throw   A.S. *thráwan,* to throw

Thra'in t' stockin'—a custom formerly practised by young people at weddings, of throwing a stocking over the shoulder at the bride and bridegroom as they sat in bed.   Whoever hit the mark was expected to be married within the year.

Thrang—busy   A.S. *thrang,* crowded   A.S. *thringan,* to press

"In helle salle be than swa gret *thrang.*"
Pricke of Conscience, l. 7364.

Threap—to contend, dispute   A.S. *threapian* O.N. *threfa*

"But tou mun ayways *threep* yen down."
Miss Blamire.   Cumb. Ball. p. 51.

"Wyth tham to *threp* that has lyfed ille here."
Pricke of Conscience, l. 5407.

Throo or Thruff—a through is a stone of such a length that when in building a wall it projects on each side ; their use is to bind or give solidity to the structure

"Then girt Joe Bruff gat on a *thruff,*
An' rais'd a fearfu' rout."
John Stagg.   Cumb. Ball. p. 194.

Thropple—the throat, or windpipe   A.S. *throt-bolla*

Throp's-wife,—an apocryphal personage who was said to be always throng, or busy, giving rise to the common phrase "As thrang as *Throp's wife*," evidently a corruption of *Thorpe's* wife

Thrums—the ends of thread, or yarn   Icel. *thrömr*, an edge   Germ. *trumm*   Du. *drom*, the end of a thing

Thrush-louse—the wood louse (*Oniscus*), a crustacean of the order *Isopoda*

Thud—a heavy fall or blow; from the sound, same as thump and bump   A.S. *thoden*

Thumpin—anything very large; a beating

Thunner—thunder   A.S. *thuner*

> "Boh th' hairy mon had miss'd my thowt,
>   An' th' clog fair crackt by th' *thunner* bowt."
>   *Waugh.*   Sketches of Lanc. Life, p. 103.

Tice—to induce, to tempt; an abbreviation of entice

> "Adam ansuerd with wykyd wyll
>   The eddyre *tysed* me theretyll."
>   *Hall. Dict.*

Tickle-tail—a loose woman

> "Heo is *Tikel* of hire *Tayl*."
>   *Piers Plowman*, Text A, Pass. iii. l. 126.

Tickle-tail—a birch rod

Tift—bodily condition   "I'se in rare *tift* fer owte ta-day."

Tifter—a hurry, bustle, as "Du it quietly now, an' don't be i' sic a *tifter* ower it."

Tiftin—breathing hard, as "It's geen me a *tiftin* clim'in that hill; it's sooa brant."

Tike—a cur dog; also frequently applied to an odd or queer fellow

"Sw. D. *tik*, f. a bitch, a foolish woman; m. a hound, a senseless lout of a man."—*Atkinson.*

"Hewe downe hertly yon heythene *tykes*."
Morte Arthure, 1. 3643.

Tilt—to incline or overturn   A.S. *tealtian*, to lean over

"The trestes *tylt* to the woze & the table bothe."
Allit. P. B. l. 832.

Tinny-winny—very small; a reduplicative form of tiny.   Dan. *tynd*, thin, small

Titter—sooner, quicker   O.N. *titt*, soon

"That if a man mught properly se his sýn
In the kynd lyknes that it falles be in,
He shuld for ferdnes *titter* it fle
Than any devel that he mught se."
Pricke of Conscience, ll. 2352-5.

"For t' time flang by at sic a reate,
Titter nor wings o' birds."
Stanyan Bigg.   Shifting Scenes, p. 171.

Tittivate—to dress up

T'll—to   A.S. and Icel. *til*

"Ther wos ol'as a lot 'at fuddled away on t' market-day neets *t'll* quite leeat afooar they went yam."
Lebby Beck Dobby, p. 5.

Toar—to struggle through a difficulty; to drag on through a weary life   Fr. *touer*, to drag   A.S. *teón*, to tug, tow   Cf. Icel. *tóra*, to live poorly

"So Betty wur laft to *toar* on bi hersel;
An' heaw hoo poo'd throo it no mortal can tell."
Waugh.   Tufts of Heather, p. 220.

Tod—the fox   Icel. *toa, tove*

Toit—to turn over, upset ; a small vessel
heeling to one side, was said by a Furness woman to
be "gaan èt *toit*." Cf. Eng. *totter*, *toddle*

Tootin—peeping, spying about   O.E. *tote*,
to spy about
"Whow myght tou in thine brother eighe· a bare mote
loken,
And in thyn owen eighe· nought a bem *toten*."
            Piers Plowman's Crede, ll. 141-42.

Toothanegg—a kind of pewter of which tea-
pots and spoons are made   Dan. *tuttenage*   "A name
given in India to zinc or spelter."—*Brande*.

Topper—surpassingly great, better than common   O.N. *toppr*, see next word
        " Eawr Tummy's taen to preitchin'—
        He's a *topper* at it too."
                Waugh.   Lanc. Songs, p. 48.

Toppin—the hair growing just above the forehead on man or animals   A.S. *top*, a tuft at the top
of anything
        "The tayle & his *toppyng* twynnen of a sute."
        Sir Gaw. & Green Knt.   Sp. E. Eng. p. 226.
        "Sup, an' straighten that reawsty *toppin*' o' thine."
                Waugh.   Tufts of Heather, p. 211.

Toppins—the top sods, cut of moss-land, used
for burning

Topple—to overturn, to tumble

Torfel—to die

Tormentle—an astringent herb, generally
found on mossy land   Dan. *tormentil*

Totterin—unsteady, ready to fall
  "Toterynge, or waverynge, *vacillacio.*"
                                    Prompt. Parv.

Touch-an-catch—the children's game of tick
  or tig

Trail—to walk lazily, to drag the feet along
  the ground   Fr. *tirailler*, to drag   Du. *treylen*, to
  draw with a rope
  "An' *trailin'* abeawt, like a hen at's i'th meawt."
                          Waugh.   Lanc. Songs, p. 28.

Tram—a cart shaft   Su. G. *traam*, a small
  log of wood

Trapes—a dirty slovenly female

Trapesin—walking about idly without an object in view   Germ. *traben*   Du. *trappen*, to tramp

Trennle—to roll anything along the ground
  A.S. *trendl*, a ball   Dan. *trumle*, to roll
    "On huyle ther perle hit *trendeled* doun."
                                    Allit. P. A. l. 41.

Trinkle—to trickle, or run slowly

Trollops—a dirty person   Germ. *trolle*, a trull,
  from *trollen*, to stroll   Cf. *trull*

Trouf—a trough, as pig-*trouf*, horse-*trouf*, etc.
  A.S. *trog, troh*   Dan. *trug*

Trounce—a weary journey.   "We wor lost
  on t' moor, an' hed a bonny *trounce* afore we gat
  yam."

Trouncin—a severe beating

Trull—a dirty woman, a strumpet Cf. *Trollops*

Trunnel—the axle of a barrow wheel A.
trendl, anything round

Trunlins—sheep droppings   A.S. *trendl*

Tummle—to fall, tumble Dan. *tumle*
tumla

Twang—a peculiar accent or intonation
the voice, as "I cud tell by his *twang* he wosn'
Forness fella."

Twitch—to pull or jerk suddenly A.S. *twicc*

Twitters—to be in a state of tremulous s
pense Cf. Germ. *zittern*, to tremble

Type—to overturn, to tumble, metaphorica
to die
" & *type* doun yonder toun when hit turned were.
                              Allit. P. C. L 5
"Th' owd lad *typ't* o'er abeawt ten o'clock
forenoon."—*Waugh.* Tufts of Heather, p. 74.

Unforbiddan—disobedient   A.S. *un*, not, a
forbiddan, to forbid. "Thou's a varra *unforbid*
barne."

Uphod—uphold, to guarantee that a pers
will do anything, as "I'll *uphod* the' he'll du it."

Up-on-end—to recover from sickness. "I w
varra badly for a while, but I've gitten *upon*
again."

Upsadoun—upside down
"And he turnyde *upsodoun* the boordis of chaunge
and the chaieris of men sellinge culueris."
                    Gosp. of Mark (*Wycliffe's*), c. xi. v.

Upshot—result, consequence, end of an affair
"He gat on t' spree, an' t' *upshot* wos 'at they lock'd him up i' t' black-hooal o' neet."

Upsides—to serve a person out, to give a "Rowland for an Oliver." "I'll sarra the' owt; thou'll see I'll be *upsides* wi' the' some day."

Uptak—the fixed price of anything, the money being laid down the object can be taken up; also a sum given for the uptaking or finding of an article of value

Varjus—verjuice, acid liquor expressed from crab-apples, hence the phrase, "As sour as crab *varjus.*" Fr. *verjus*, *vert*, green and *jus*, juice

Varra—very
"We greeave a lock a peeats a top a t'fell ez cuz in *varra* weel fer eldin."—*Sp. West. Dialect*, p. 1.

Varsal—universal. "Ther niver wos his marra i' o' this *varsal* ward (world)."

Vogue—way, mode or fashion   Ital. *voga*, mode, fashion

Waad—to wade through water, snow, or grass A.S. *wád*, a ford; *wádan*, to wade Du. *waaden* Dan. *vaad*, wet

Waaken—to awake from sleep, to rouse up from inaction Du. *waaken* Dan. *vække*, to awake, incite A.S. *wacan*, *wæcan*, to move, to awake "Thou is a slairin thing; thou wants *waakenin* up."

Waar—to lay out money, to spend W. *gwario*, to spend "Mind thou dusn't *waar* o' the brass afoore thou gits yam."
"Then a thowt, what a mun *waar* summat fer my mudther."—*Sp. West. Dialect*, p. 18.

Waar—worse Dan. *værre* A.S. *wærra*, worse "He's varra badly, I think he's *waar* ta-day ner common."

Waar—where, in which place A.S. *hwar* Du. *waar*

"*Whaar* did ta find 'em? said t' judge. I' t' toppin mow, sed t' lad."—*Lonsdale Mag.* v. 2, p. 90.

Wabble—unsteady, to hobble in walking; a top, just before it ceases spinning, *wabbles. Webster* says of this word, "It's place can not be supplied by any other word in the language. It is neither low nor barbarous." W. *gwibio*, to move in a circular form

Waffy—weak, tasteless, insipid food; a feeling of faintness
"Weffe, *vapor.*"—*Prompt. Parv.*

Waggle—to shake, move, wag A.S. *wágian* Du. *waggelen* Dan. *vakle*, to sit loose, wag

Walla—insipid Cf. *Welshed* "These poddish er varra *walla;* ther's neaa saut i' them." O.E. *walle* or *walcw*, nauseous Cf. Du. *walgen*, to loathe, turn the stomach
"Venim or vernish· or vinegre, I trowe,
Walleth in my wombe· or waxeth, ich wene."
Piers Plowman, Text A, Pass. v. ll. 70-1.

Wallop—to flog; to flap with anything soft
"A *wallop* ower t' lug."

Wamp—wasp

Wan—won, gained a contest

"For, by hym that al thys world *wan!*
Thou hast makyd me a man."
Rel. Ant. v. 2, p. 88.
"Perkyn *wan* five, and Hud *wan* twa."
Turn. of Tott. Percy's Rel. p. 94.

Wandle—slim, straight, slender, wandy

Wang-tooth—a molar, jaw tooth   A.S. *wang*,
cheek, jaw   O.Sw. *wang*
   "Wange Toothe *molaris*."—*Prompt. Parv.*
   "Men might haue sen through both his chekes,
      And euery *wang-toth* and where it sat."
            Note to l. 421 *Piers Plow. Crede*, ed. Skeat.
   "And out of this ass's cheke, that was so dreye,
      Out of a *woung-toth* sprong anon a welle."
                  Cant. Tales, l. 15530.

Wankle—weakly, unstable   A.S. *wancol*, unsteady   Germ. *wankel*
Mr. Atkinson, in his *Gloss. Clevl. Dial.*, quotes the
following from *Layamon's Brut* (iii. 280)—
   "quelen tha ældren :   died the elder,
   quelen tha yeongere :   died the younger,
   qlæn tha wifmen :   died the women,
   quelen tha *wanclen* :   died the *wancle*."
"That barne's terble *wankle* on its legs," is a very
common expression in Furness.

Ward—world   A.S. *weorold, woruld*, the world
Dan. *verden*
   "For in the *ward* it was the maner tho."
            Lancelot of the Laik, ed. Skeat, l. 3184.
   "An' sich cawve tales as *Cornish Peter*, at fund a
new *ward*."—*Tim Bobbin*, preface 3rd ed.

Warda'—a week day, any day but Sunday
Suio. Goth. *hwardag*   Dan. *hverdag*, every day,
   "*hverdags* klæder," ordinary, common clothes

Wark—work, labour   A.S. *wearc*   Dan. *verk*
   "An' then, efter duin his *wark*, he wod ga an' see
t' priest."—*Lebby Beck Dobby*, p. 4.
   "Thae's getten thi *wark* bi th' hond."
               Waugh. Tufts of Heather, p. 318.

Wark—to ache, generally applied to a shooting
pain as the head-ache or tooth-ache.   "Werkyn, or
heed akyn. *Doleo*,"—*Prompt. Parv.*   In a note
Mr. Way quotes "*Cephalia* est humor capitis,
Anglice the hedde warke." ORTUS.   "The Hede-
warke, *Cephalia, cephalargia* CATH. ANG." A.S.
weorcan Dan. *verke*, to pain, smart

" Now full to the thropple, wi' head-*warks* and heart-
    aches,   .
Some crap to the clock-kease instead o' the dure."
                Anderson.   Cumb. Ball. p. 340.

Warm—to beat

Warse—worse ; wars, warse   Moes. G. *wairs*

" Of life and deth nowe chuse the,
    There is the woman, here is the galowe tree ;
    Of boothe choyce harde is the parte ;
    The woman is the *warsse*, drive forthe the carte."
                Rel. Ant. v. I, p. 288.

Waster or Wastrel—a spendthrift, anything
    cast away as useless, a useless fellow   A.S. *wéstan*,
    to waste

" He bad *wastors* go worche· what thei best couthe."
        Piers Plow. ed. Skeat, Text A, Pass. v. l. 24.
        "From *wastors* and wikkede men."
                . *Ibid.,* Pass. vii. l. 31.
        " And alle suche *waisters* as he wasse."
                Sir Amadace, st. xxi. l. 8.

Watter—water, a lake, tarn, as Coniston
    watter, Windermere *watter*, Elter-*watter*, etc. Dan.
    vater A.S. *wæter*

        " And alle *watters* als thai sal rynne."
                Pricke of Conscience, l. 4777.
" And made William to weope· *watur* with his eyen."
        Piers Plow. ed. Skeat, Text A, Pass. v. l. 44.

Watter-brash—watery eructations of an acid character Dan. *vater*, water, and *brække sig*, to vomit, disgorge

Wax—to grow, increase O.N. *vaxa* Sw. *växa* A.S. *weaxan*

" *Waxyn*, or growyn. *Cresco, accresco*."
Prompt. Parv.

Wax-kernals—glandular swellings in the neck, said to be signs of growing or waxing

" '*Glandula, nodus sub cute*, a waxynge curnelle.' MED. In Roy. M.S. 17, c. xvii. *de infirmitatibus*, are mentioned '*Glanduli*, wax kyrnel.' 'Waxyng kyrnels; *glande*, glanders. Kyrnell or knobbe in the necke, or other where, *glandre*.' PALSG. ' *Tolles*, a waxynge kernell.' ELYOT."—*Way* in Prompt. Parv. p. 276.

Wedder—weather, as wet *wedder*, dry *wedder*, etc. A.S. *weder*

"Thorw Flodes and foul *weder·* Fruites schal fayle."
Piers Plow. A, Pass. vii. l. 310.

Weel—well Dan. *vel* A.S. *wæl*

"But niver heed ; she loved me *weel*,
That's a' I care to knaw."
Stanyan Bigg. Shifting Scenes, p. 172.

Weft—support, importance, energy Cf. Dan. *vægt*, energy, weight. "He hes a deeal o' *weft* about him." "Give it some *weft*"—give it some weight

Welsh'd—suffering from insipidity of food, as " I'se fairly *welsh'd* away wi' sic walla stuff."

" Walsh, welsche, insipid, Teut. *gaelsch*, ingratus, insuavis sapore aut odore.."—*Jamieson.*

Mr. Atkinson gives "Du. *walghen*, to nauseate, loathe."—*Clev. Gloss.*

Weltin—anything very large, as a "Girt *weltin* fella."

Weme—innocent looking, quiet "Yan wodn't think he hed it in him, he looks sooa *weme*." Germ. *bequem*, easy A.S. *cwéman* O. E. *queme*, to please, satisfy

Weemless—spotless, without a fault A.S. *wem*, a spot, and *leas*, free from
> " Whilke that in-comes *wemles*,
> And ai werkes rightwisenes."
>> *Psalm* xiv. 2. Sp. E. Eng. p. 83.

Wha—who A.S. *hwá*
" Thare-fore I syghe and crye, *Wha* sall schewe to the lufede Jhesu that I langwys for lufe."
>> *Hampole's Prose Treat.* p. 2.

Whang—a thong, a shoe tie A.S. *thwang*, a leather string

Whang—a blow
> " Ned Wulson brong his lug a *whang*;
> Then owre he flew, the peats amang."
>> *Anderson.* Cumb. Ball. p. 301.

Whemmel—to turn over, to upset, knock down
" Jam. refers Sc. *quhemle, whommel*, to S. G. *hvimla*, to be giddy. I should prefer O. N. *hvelfa*, invertere, to turn upside down."—*Atkinson.* Clevel. Gloss.
" Wi' that a ups wimmi flale an fetcht him a cloot undre't lugg an *whemmelt* him slap ower it guttre."
>> *Sp. West. Dial.* p. 15.

Whewt—to whistle Cf. Dan. *flöite*, to whistle at
" *Whewt* on Tummas an Mary."
>> *Tim Bobbin*, pref. to 3rd ed.

Whin—furze, gorse *(Ulex Europæa)* W. *chwyn,* weeds

"Cotgrave gives '*genest espineux,* furres, *whinnes,* gorse, thorn-broom.'"—*Way* in Prompt. Parv.

" The *whinnes* shall prick the to the bare beane and Christ receive thy sawle."
Mirc's Instructions to Parish Priests, Note p. 91.

" He prick'lt his shins i' Wulson's *whins,*
And swore that some sud smart for't."
Mark Lonsdale. Cumb. Ball. p. 281.

Whingin—whining

" An' then she *whinged* and rooart like a lile barne."
Sp. West. Dial. p. 11.

Whisht—hush O.Fr. *houische*

" The wild waves *whist.*"
Shakspeare. Tempest, Act 1, Sc. 2.

Wisht—noiseless " *Wisht* as a mouse."

Wi—with

"Yonder's a pig i' t' roum *wi*' t' lass."
Lonsdale Mag. v. 2, p. 90.

Wibbet—wee bit, a very small child, a little piece "What a *wibbet* that barne is."

Wick—living, frisky, lively A.S. *cwic* Dan. *qvik* Du. *kwik* Sw. *qvick*

" Na *quyk* creature salle lyf than,
Bot anely aungelle, develle, and man."
Pricke of Conscience, l. 6981.

" And they had ale at towd a tale,
'T wur cool, an *wick,* an foamin."
Waugh. Tufts of Heather, p. 216.

" Sec fashions I'll ne'er follow while I'se *whick.*"
Ewan Clark. Cumb. Ball. p. 161.

Wicks—the long creeping roots of the couch grass, (*Triticum repens.*) Nothing short of actual burning will destroy their vitality

Widdy—a willow tree, a wand   Dan. *vidie* A.S. *withie*

Wig—a small oblong cake made from common dough, with the addition of a little butter, sugar, and carraway seeds

"'*Pastilla,* a cake, cracknel or *wygge.*' ORTUS. '*Eschandé,* a kind of *wigg* or symnell.' COTG. '*Wygge, Eschandé.*' PALSG. '*Wig* or bun, a bunn or little manchet; *Collyra,* libum.' GOULDM. '*Wegghe,* panis triticeus, libum oblongum.' KILIAN, Dict. Teut."—*Way* in Prompt. Parv. pp. 100, 456, & 526.

Withie or With—a willow wand   (See Widdy)

Woo—wool
" An' i' t' lang winter neets a card a bit o' *woo.*"
Sp. West. Dial. p. 1.

Wooset—worsted
" We knat quorse *wosset* stockings."
Sp. West. Dial. p. 28.

Wrang—wrong   A.S. *wrang*
"That wont watz whyle deuoyde my *wrange.*"
Allit. Poems, A, l. 15.
" Fie, Roger, fie—a sairy lass to *wrang,*
And let her all this trouble undergang."
Relph. Cumb. Ball. p. 23.

Yabble—able, wealthy
" A varra *yabble* man i' hee life wes wantan ta simma."—*Sp. West. Dial.* p. 16.

Yad or Yaud—a horse

Mr. Atkinson says—"Essentially the same word with jade."—*Clevel. Gloss.*

"Tired as a *jade* in overloaden cart."
Quoted in Webster.

"Come, Gwordie lad, unyoke the *yad*,
Let's gow to Rosley Fair."
Anderson. Cumb. Ball. p. 295.

Yak—oak A.S. *aac* Icel. *eik*

"It was nobbut a white feeac'd cow at hed its heead ower t' wo, an wos rubbin it up an down again a *yak* tree."—*Lebby Beck Dobby*, p. 4.

Yakkeran—an acorn

Yal—whole "A *yal* apple."

Yally—ten byes at football

Yam—home Cumb. *heeam* Sc. *hame* A.S. *ham*

Yan—one A.S. *án, æn* O.E. *ane* Dan. *een*

"Thus was thow aye and euer sall be,
Thre yn *ane* and *ane* yn thre."
Relig. Pieces, p. 59.

"This *ean* night this *ean* night every night and awle."
Mirc's Ins. to Parish Priests, note, p. 90.

"*Yan* o' them com up tumma, an sed he was reet fane ta simma."—*Sp. West. Dial.* p. 16.

"A borden 's leeter shared by two,
Nor when it's born by *yan*."
North Lons. Mag. p. 19.

Yance—once

"I'se off ut put owr exin's in,
Ut git it deeun at *yance*."
North Lons. Mag. p. 19.

Yan's-sel—one's-self

Yarbs—herbs   Sp. *yerba*

"There's a lot o' eggs under th' *yarbs* i' th' basket."
Waugh.   Tufts of Heather, p. 140.

Yār—hair   Dan. *haar*   Sw. *har*

"It med my *yare* ston straight up."
Waugh.   Tufts of Heather, p. 10.

Yark—to beat, switch with a stick

"Icel. *hreckia*, to beat, *jarke*, pes feriens."
Jamieson.

Mr. Atkinson thinks "O.N. *hiacka, jacka,* lies nearer the root."—*Clevel. Gloss.*

"Thou needn't glime, I'll *yark* thy hide."
John Stagg.   Cumb. Ball. p. 226.

Yarkin—a beating

Yean—to lamb   A.S. *eanian*

Yerth-fast—a boulder stone deeply seated in the earth

Yow—a female sheep, an ewe   A.S. *eowu* Du. *ouwe*

Yower—the udder of a cow   "O.N. *júgr, júfr, júr* Dan. *yver* Sw. *jufver* Sw. D. *gur, jaur.*"
Atkinson.

THE END.

GEO. COWARD, PRINTER, SCOTCH STREET, CARLISLE.

The SONGS and BALLADS of CUMBERLAND;

with Biographical Sketches, Notes, and Glossary. Edited by Sidney Gilpin. With Portrait of Miss Blamire.

(A New Edition in preparation.)

One of the most interesting collections of poetry which have been lately published is the "Songs and Ballads of Cumberland." How many people know anything of Miss Blamire? Yet she was the author of that most beautiful and pathetic of ballads beginning, "And ye shall walk in silk attire." Every one will, therefore, thank the editor for the conscientous way in which he has issued her pieces, and given us some account of her life. It was she, too, who wrote that other beautiful ballad, worthy of Lady Anne Lindsay, "What ails this heart o' mine?" which, in our opinion, is poetry full of truth and tenderness. Indeed, we should be disposed to look upon it as a critical touchstone, and to say that those who did not like it could not possibly appreciate true poetry. . . . We can only advise the reader to buy the book, and we feel sure that he, like ourselves, will be thankful to the editor. —*Westminster Review.*

We like the Cumberland Songs a good deal better than the Lancashire ones which we reviewed a fortnight back. There is more go and more variety in them; the hill-air makes them fresher, and we do not wonder that Mr. Gilpin feels—now he has got "tem put in prent"—
Aw England cannot bang them.
We certainly cannot recollect a better collection. . .. While the author of "Joe and the Geologist" lives, we shall rest assured that the Cumberland dialect will be well represented in verse as well as prose, though we suppose he cannot love to describe the roaring scenes at weddings and the like that his predecessors witnessed. . . . The dialect is rich in reduplicated words—in good forms—in old English words; and the volume altogether is one that should find a place on the shelf of every reader of poetry and student of manners, customs, and language.—*The Reader.*

The truly Cumbrian minstrel towards the close of the last century seems to have approached the Scotch in his pictures of rural courtship, and to have been still greater in his descriptions of weddings, as of some other festivities of a more peculiar character. He had a healthy and robust standard of feminine beauty, and his most riotous mirth was more athletic and less purely alcoholic than that which flourished in Burns's native soil.—*The Spectator.*